# THE KNOWLEDGE

# THE KNOWLEDGE

A Man's Guide To Dating
In The Digital Age

David Slater

Copyright © 2023 by David Slater

All rights reserved.

No part of this book may be reproduced in any form or by any electronic or mechanical means, including information storage and retrieval systems, without written permission from the author, except for the use of brief quotations in a book review.

ISBN: 978-1-7393655-0-9

www.datingknowledge.co.uk

# Contents

Preface / ix
Introduction / xii

Part 1
## What Do Women Want? / 1
Attraction Isn't A Choice / 5
What Do Men Find Attractive? / 6
What Do Women Find Attractive? / 7
Provision & Protection / 8
Non-Physical Traits / 9
Women And Age / 11
Changing Preferences / 13
Hypergamy / 14
Mimetic Desire / 16
Chapter Summary / 18

Part 2
## Becoming A Desirable Man / 19
Dress To Impress / 22
Exercise / 28
Diet / 32
Physical Appearance / 34
Wealth / 37
Interests / 38
Happiness / 39
Confidence / 42
Chapter Summary / 47

Contents

Part 3
### Online Dating / 49
   A Brief History Of Online Dating / 52
   The Pros And Cons Of Online Dating / 54
   Which Platforms Are Right For You? / 61
   Creating A Great Profile / 64
   A Picture Paints A Thousand Words / 65
   Writing Your Profile / 67
   Chapter Summary / 71

Part 4
### Messaging Strategy / 73
   The Five Terrible Opening Gambits / 76
   Impactful Openers / 79
   How To Succeed With Impactful Openers / 83
   Introduction To Conversations / 87
   The Queue / 88
   Conversational Stages And Objectives / 93
   Mastering Conversations / 100
   Chapter Summary / 106

Part 5
### Meeting In Person / 109
   Basic Dating Logistics / 112
   Creating A Scene / 114
   Building Attraction / 118
   After The First Date / 136
   General Dating Advice / 140
   Chapter Summary / 148

Part 6
### Dating Mastery / 149
   Terrible Dating Advice / 152
   Embracing Failure / 165

Take A Break / 166
Exceptions To The Rule / 168
Notes To A Young Man / 169
What Is Dating Mastery? / 173

Epilogue / 175

# Preface

Various studies from across the globe paint the same dire picture - men's love lives are in decline. Over the past few decades men are now more likely: to be currently single, to have never been in a relationship, to lose their virginity older, and to remain sexless throughout life.

There are a myriad of reasons for this, not least of which women today have more freedom and choice when it comes to selecting partners. They don't have to 'settle down' through economic necessity, nor are they restricted to the dozen or so eligible men they know through friends/family/work/socialising.

The 'digital age' has made it easier than ever before to meet strangers and form romantic relationships. But not everyone has benefitted from this technological revolution. Faced with a new dating environment, many men are failing to find a partner and love.

This book aims to address that.

Over the past twenty years or so, I've had great success in my love life. I've been able to arrange multiple dates each week with beautiful, intelligent women; week in, week out. I have dated accomplished women from: Oxbridge graduates, doctors, Magic Circle lawyers, prestigious tech firm executives, millionaires, and even aristocrats.
Over the years, these dates have resulted in short term flings, long term relationships, and life-long friendships.

I know immediately what you're thinking: *"Well Dave, you're obviously very attractive and/or wealthy..."*

## Preface

Far from it. My background isn't what you'd expect from a man with this track record.

- I am not handsome. Besides my mother, I don't think a single woman in my life has commented on my good looks. As a child I was bullied relentlessly for my facial features. In my early twenties I started to lose my hair - the only part of my physical appearance I was content with.

- From the ages of 11 to 18, I'd attended an all boys school. Besides family, I had absolutely no interaction with girls my age during that time. Due to this lack of exposure, I was very nervous and awkward around women as I became an adult.

- I am not a social butterfly. I find social interactions, especially with groups, stressful and draining after a while. I'm notorious amongst friends and family for sneaking away from gatherings at the earliest opportunity.

- I am not wealthy. I come from a working class family, I didn't attended university, and I've always earned around, or just below, the average UK salary.

Not exactly attributes you associate with a Casanova: I'm no Adonis, I'm not the life and soul of any party, and I certainly don't frequent Verbier for ski getaways.

So how did I attract all these women? Through years of trial and error. My dating success came slowly but surely as I learnt what worked and what didn't. At the beginning I was utterly hopeless. I couldn't attract anyone's attention, let alone the type of woman I was hoping to meet. But through perseverance I became something of an expert on the dating game.

And I want to share that expertise with you. I've managed to punch well above my weight when it comes to attracting women, and I can help you do the same.

So if you're mystified by the opposite sex and struggling to find that special someone, you've come to the right place. This book contains a treasure trove of information that will help you create a flourishing love life and find the happiness you deserve.

# Introduction

The drive for romantic companionship is hardwired into us, like the need to eat or to sleep. But unlike making a sandwich or retiring to bed, acquiring a partner isn't intuitive or easy for most men. To make matters worse, there's a stigma around learning how to attract women; that somehow you've failed as a man if that ability doesn't come naturally.

Put that thought out of your mind immediately. Courtship is a complex undertaking few men have a natural aptitude for. Like any skill, it requires a great deal of insight, study and practice to master.
This book will provide the most effective route to that mastery.

The Dating Knowledge Pyramid represents all the learning required to find love in the 'digital age'.

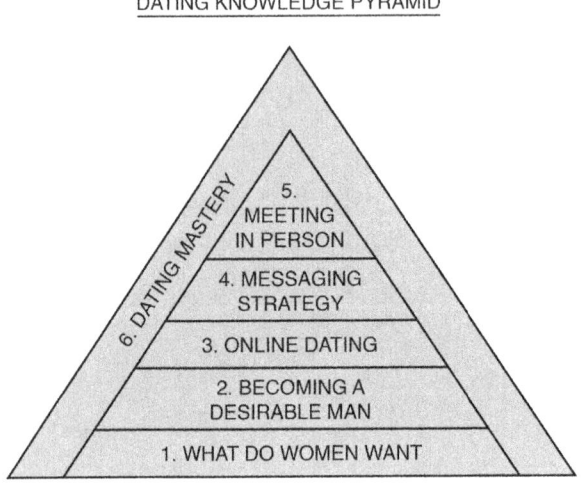

Introduction

Over the course of this book you will learn:

- The psychology behind attraction and what exactly women look for in a man.
- How to become a desirable man by enhancing your life and becoming the best version of yourself.
- A detailed guide to online dating and how to create an alluring profile.
- What to say in an introductory message, how to establish a conversation, and how to secure a date.
- Exactly what to do during a date to build attraction and establish a lasting romantic connection.

> ### *Personal Experience*
> Throughout the book I'll also be sharing my own personal experiences - anecdotes highlighting how I'd learnt or applied certain knowledge and strategies.

Let's begin at the foundation of our pyramid by asking the most crucial question: what exactly do women want?

# What Do Women Want?

What Do Women Want

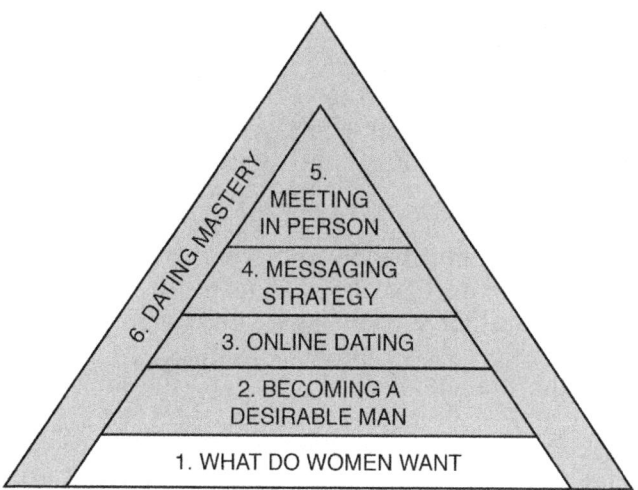

*"The great question that has never been answered, and which I have not yet been able to answer, despite my thirty years of research into the feminine soul, is 'What does a woman want?'"*

>   Sigmund Freud
>   founder of psychoanalysis

A century after Freud's "great unanswered question" most of us still consider women something of a mystery. Especially when it comes to how they choose their partners. Attractive women, who have their pick of men, are quite happy to pair up with some rather questionable types. You'll find beautiful women with men who are:

- Ugly
- Old enough to be their father
- Poor
- Obese, or otherwise unhealthy
- Addicted to drugs, drink, gambling etc

- Known to be unfaithful
- Violent

And a whole list of other characteristics most of us would actively avoid in a woman, no matter what compensatory factors are in play.

Given the above, and maybe from your own experience, you may believe women have terrible taste in men. They don't. Woman are excellent at choosing quality partners. If it weren't for their selection skills, humans wouldn't be the dominant species on this planet.

Women's choice in partners makes perfect sense once you understand the science behind attraction. Only after learning what women find attractive, can you hope to increase your own desirability and have success with the opposite sex.

# Attraction Isn't A Choice

Perhaps the most important factor to understand with attraction is that it isn't a conscious decision. A woman has as much control over who and what she finds attractive as you do; practically none at all. The feeling of attraction is an automatic response, just like feeling hungry, or cold, or tired. You don't choose to have those feelings, they occur naturally under certain criteria.

It's important to internalise this for a couple of reasons. Firstly, it will help you accept rejection without taking it personally. If a woman doesn't reciprocate your feelings, it's not a conscious decision. She literally can't help it. She isn't actively deciding to not like you, it just is what it is.

Secondly, and on a more positive note, if you follow the advice in this book you will automatically become more attractive. Women will want to date you and be with you. They won't be able to help themselves; it will be an unconscious, unwitting feeling on their part.

# What Do Men Find Attractive?

Presumably Freud didn't have any trouble knowing what men wanted. It's fairly simple, even if it's not something we articulate to ourselves.
In a word: reproduction. Subconsciously, we are looking to pass on our genes. We look for women who offer the best indicators of producing superior offspring.

The most attractive women:

- Are younger, rather than older. A woman's fertility peaks in her early to mid twenties and declines after this.
- Have symmetrical facial features and body, resulting from good genes.
- Regardless of age, have physical features that denote youth (skin clear of blemishes and wrinkles, healthy head of hair, full lips, firm breasts, etc)
- Have slim waists with wider hips, correlating with good health and fertility

These are the cornerstones of a desirable woman. Everything else (breast size, height, hair/eye colour, etc) is a personal preference, not universal.

What we find most attractive in women are their physical characteristics. No matter a man's status in life (young or old, rich or poor), he will always find the same type of woman most preferable. Those markers of producing superior offspring are a constant, and paramount, attraction for us.

# What Do Women Find Attractive?

Like us, women also find the signals of good genes (and therefore superior offspring) attractive. In men these traits include:

- General good health indicators (not overweight, clear skin, etc)
- Symmetrical face and body
- Masculine facial features (wider jaw, square chin, etc)
- Muscular (fit and strong, not necessarily extreme "bodybuilder" types)
- Broad shoulders and slim waist (the torso "V" shape)
- Height - taller rather than shorter

But for women, physical characteristics are only one part of the attraction puzzle. A man is more than just a potential sperm donor: he can also be a provider and a protector. These traits can be equally, if not more valuable than a man's looks.

# Provision & Protection

Today's independent, self-sufficient women are an entirely new phenomenon in our species history. In The West at least, a woman enjoys the same freedoms as any man. She can study any subject at any university, can pursue any career in any industry, and succeed in whatever path she chooses.

As a result, this generation of women do not depend on a man to provide, nor protect her from the outside world.

For the previous hundreds of thousands of years, this wasn't the case. In prehistoric times, women were dependent on men to hunt and gather food, and to protect them and their offspring from predators and other humans. In living memory, women were still dependant on men to work and provide them with food and shelter.

These traits in a man, the ability to provide and protect, were vital to women. It's no surprise then they are biologically programmed to find them attractive.

So what exactly are these provider/protector traits in men? Some of them actually link back to our physical characteristics. A tall, muscular man is better able to protect her from threats than a shorter, less muscular one. A fit man in good health is better able to do work and provide for her than an unfit, ill one.

But there are many traits women seek in men that have nothing to do with our physicality.

# Non-Physical Traits

### Money

The most obvious non-physical trait women seek in men is wealth. Money is the foundation to our survival. With it, you can secure food, shelter, medical care, and the freedom to do what you want in life. The more money you have, the better provider you'll be.

Indicators of wealth are attractive. Few women would turn down a serious date from a man who drives a Ferarri and lives in a Mayfair penthouse, no matter what he looks like.

Physical possessions aren't the only indicators of wealth. Where you were born and raised; your education; accent and mannerisms; interests and hobbies; where you go on holiday, are all financial clues and can be attractive traits.

### Status

This ties in somewhat with money but not always. Status is determined by your position in any given hierarchy, and how much respect that earns from others.

One's profession is a major contributing factor. Some careers have high status due to earning potential: finance, law, and tech for example. Others due to their value to society or bravery required to perform the role. Firefighters and police officers are rarely considered wealthy, but are highly respected.

High social standing amongst any group is an attractive trait. If your hobby was creating YouTube videos on the intricacies of the Victorian railway network, that in itself isn't particularly

attractive. But if you were a world leading expert in that subject and your videos were enjoyed by millions of people across the world, that is attractive. You have status.
Status is synonymous with importance, and important men are better able to provide for, and protect their partner and family.

## Intelligence

'Sapiosexual' is now a fashionable dating term. It describes a person who is sexually attracted to intelligence. There's good reason smarter men are considered attractive. A high IQ correlates with several benefits, including increased earnings and career prospects, better general health and a longer lifespan.

In the past century, social mobility has dramatically changed for intellectuals. In days gone by, if you were born into a poor farming family, it didn't matter how smart you were. You were going to be a farmer just like your father, and like his father before him.

Now, the richest men in the world are tech billionaires who have created the world's IT and internet infrastructure. Their extreme wealth wasn't inherited: they'd put their intellect to good use and reaped the rewards.
In a meritocratic society, there is a strong correlation between intelligence and the ability to provide.

## Confidence/Self-Esteem

These attributes exist in men who feel comfortable or competent. Think of a scenario that would make you nervous. It could be administering first aid to a serious injury, giving a speech to hundreds of strangers, or even approaching an attractive woman at a bar.

Now imagine you've already performed this scenario hundreds of times before with no issues. You wouldn't be nervous at all. You'd feel self-assured and at ease. This feeling comes from experience and success.

This is what makes confidence attractive. It's indicative of a man who knows what he's doing, and succeeds in what he does.

### Humour

A good sense of humour encompasses several attractive traits. It displays intelligence; the ability to articulate original, abstract ideas. It also shows confidence; the ability to communicate clearly and put one's self forward as the centre of attention. Funny people are also well thought of and liked by others; they possess a high status amongst groups.

### Caring

The above traits show a woman you have the ability, or at least the potential, to provide and protect but that's no good if you choose not to. There's no benefit to marrying a multimillionaire if he's a Scrooge and chooses to hide his wealth and live frugally.
A generous nature and the ability to think of other's wellbeing show a man is willing to exercise his power to provide and protect those around him.

# Women and Age

I've mentioned a man's preference in women is consistent throughout his life: young and beautiful is always most attractive.

For women there is no constant. What they find most attractive evolves over time. A woman's preferences at

## What Do Women Want

eighteen years old are completely different when she reaches thirty-eight.

The most obvious difference is a partner's optimal age. To any man, the ideal woman is in her twenties. It's at this stage of life she's at her most fertile.

But fertility isn't such a time sensitive issue for men. Post-puberty, a man is potentially fertile for the rest of his days. This is one of the reasons men don't reach a peak attractiveness at any particular age.

For women, a man's ideal age is roughly the same age as herself. Statistics show younger women (twenty to thirty years) prefer a man slightly older than herself, whereas older women (forty and up) prefer a man slightly younger to herself. But either way, as a woman ages, so does her ideal partner.

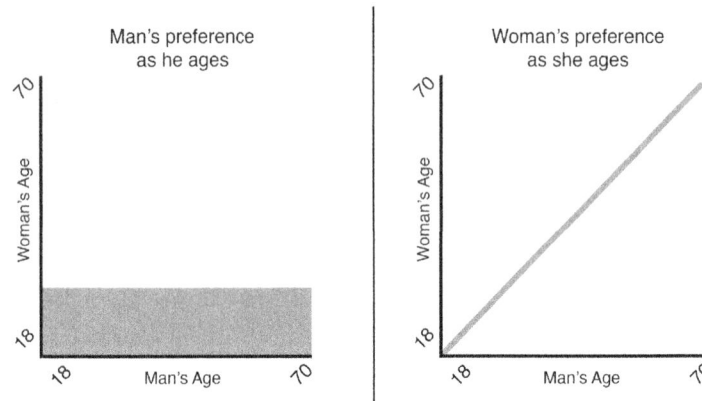

## Changing Preferences

As discussed, a man has two types of attractive qualities: what he looks like (facial features, height, masculinity, etc), and who he is (job/career, wealth, status, sense of humour, etc).

These two categories aren't equally attractive to women. Their importance is determined by a woman's age and her circumstances.

Generally speaking, when women are younger and most fertile, they find physical characteristics in men most alluring. An 18-year-old doesn't care so much if a guy has a steady job at the bank and is looking at promotion next year. She's most interested in how hot he is.
For the 38-year-old, if he's hot or not isn't such a deal-breaker, but his career in banking is now an attractive quality.

As women age, their attraction to physical characteristics decreases, whilst their attraction to the provider/protector qualities increase. Generally, once a woman reaches 30 or so, those latter qualities become more important than what a man looks like.

This isn't to say younger women have absolutely no interest in provider/protector qualities, and older women are happy to partner up with a gargoyle so long as he has a decent job. It's just that over time, there is a significant shift in what's most appealing.

Men who occupy the extremes are always desirable, no matter what a woman's age or situation. A devastatingly handsome, 6ft6 Adonis will always be sought after, even if his personal life is a mess and he doesn't have a penny to his name.

Conversely, a balding, obese, 5ft2 billionaire will have no issue attracting beautiful women.

A woman's circumstances also determine her preferences in men. Independently wealthy women have little need for a provider, so a handsome man is a higher priority no matter her age. On the other hand, a 20-year-old in need of provision/protection (a single mother perhaps, or from a poor background) will put more stock in a partner who can improve her circumstances.

# Hypergamy

Hypergamy was a term first coined in the 19th century to describe the Hindu practice of women 'marrying up'. India then had a very strict caste system, where one's social status was determined at birth. The only way to escape this status, which for many meant a lifetime of poverty, was to marry a man in the class above.

Understandably, higher caste men were the preference for women seeking a partner. Social scientists have found hypergamy doesn't just apply to 19th century Hindus. Women generally have a strong preference for 'marrying up'.

In practical terms, this means women seek men who are in a league above their own. This could mean a man who earns more money than she does, a man from a better background than hers, or a man who is more physically attractive than she is.

Remember, hypergamy works in relative terms, not absolute. By this I mean a white collar professional who earns a six-figure salary is in an advantageous position when it comes to dating almost any woman. However, if his prospective date is

What Do Women Want

an entrepreneur who earns millions a year from her amazing business skills, she won't be so impressed.

Hypergamy doesn't just stop once a relationship's established. If, during their time together, a man's position lowers relative to his partners (say his career prospects decline, or hers significantly increase), her attraction to him will decrease accordingly.

HYPERGAMIC FEMALE ATTRACTION

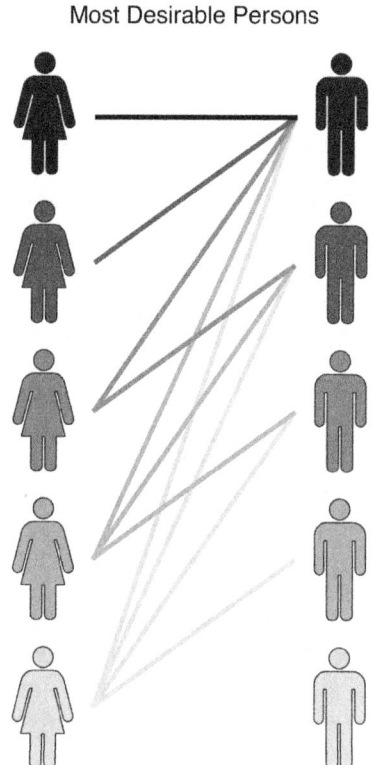

15

# Mimetic Desire

Having read this far, you're now better informed on the opposite sex than 99% of your fellow men. There is one more attraction concept worth understanding - mimetic desire.

This is a term coined by French polymath René Girard in the 1970s. Girard proposed a theory to explain why we value certain things. He stated: *"Man is the creature who does not know what to desire, and he turns to others in order to make up his mind. We desire what others desire because we imitate their desires."*

In layman's terms, he's describing the bandwagon effect, where we want things because they are desirable to other people. This concept holds true for attracting the opposite sex. A woman will find a man attractive if he is sought after by other women.

Think on this scenario. A physically unattractive man walks into a bar alone. He's noticed by women at the venue and promptly ignored. Now what if the same man enters the bar, but is accompanied by two very attractive women. The women are flirty with him, and obviously aren't just friends.

Suddenly he has status. It's not obvious why he has two hot women on his arm. He could be seriously rich, or a celebrity of some sorts? It doesn't matter to the women observing him at the bar. He's now an intriguing and attractive prospect - because he's desired by other women.

Swap the genders and the scenario wouldn't work. A physically unattractive women entering a bar with two hot men wouldn't make her any more attractive to the men already in the bar. They'd notice the trio and probably think: *"That's odd..."*

So think of mimetic desire as a compounding effect: once you're attractive to some women, you're automatically desirable to more.

### *Personal Experience*

In my late teens and early twenties I socialised with a group of friends. There were around twenty of us, a mixture of guys and girls. Most of the guys I'd gone to school with, and the girls were friends of friends who'd joined our group over time. On any given night, I could visit the local pub and know that at least a few of the gang would be there. The girls were friendly, but never showed interest in me romantically.

That changed when I met my first proper girlfriend. Now off the market and in a relationship, suddenly I wasn't invisible to the girls anymore. A couple then expressed interest, and one was trying to set me up with a female friend - despite knowing I was taken.

Nothing about me changed: same appearance, same job. I wasn't suddenly 'confident' or giving off different vibes. Their interest in me seemed purely due to me now having a girlfriend.

Years later, a friend capitalised on mimetic desire by wearing a wedding ring when socialising, despite being single. He was convinced women gave him more attention with it on - and he was probably right.

## Chapter Summary

- Sexual attraction is an automatic response to certain stimuli. It is not a conscious choice. You cannot *decide* to find someone attractive or unattractive.

- Men are almost exclusively attracted to signs of fertility in women. These signs are physical characteristics. Namely: youth, body size and shape, symmetry and good health.

- Women are attracted to physical characteristics in men, but they also desire men who are able to provide for and protect them.

- These provision/protection signals in men include wealth and status. These signals have subsidiary traits, namely intelligence, humour and kindness.

- Men are most attracted to young, fertile women, no matter the man's age. Women are most attracted to men around their own age.

- As women mature, their preference for physically attractive men is less prominent. Instead, they prefer men better able to provide and protect.

- Women will always prefer to 'marry up' - that is, partner up with a man of higher social standing/richer/physically more attractive than she is.

- Women are automatically attracted to men whom other women desire.

PART 2

# Becoming A Desirable Man

*"The fight is won or lost far away from witnesses - behind the lines, in the gym, and out there on the road, long before I dance under those lights."*

    Muhammed Ali
    heavyweight world champion boxer

In one respect, a date is much like Ali's description of a boxing match. The outcome may be decided long before you even meet a prospective paramour. It doesn't matter what you say and do during your time together if you've not put in the work prior to meeting.

Before pursuing dates and meeting women, you must work on becoming a desirable man. Once you've achieved this, everything else falls into place and you'll be spared the disheartening failure most men experience when looking for love.

We've seen in the previous chapter what women find attractive. Broadly speaking: what you look like, and your ability to provide and protect.

# Dress To Impress

When it comes to attraction, looks aren't the only criteria for enticing women. However, that's not to say physical appearance is not important. For the best results with women, you must become as handsome as possible.

There are many practical ways to achieve this. The quickest and easiest is through clothing.

Psychologists have studied the relationship between what we wear and how others perceive us.
In one experiment, female participants were shown several images of handsome male models. The models were dressed in a variety of outfits, from casual gear (jeans, trainers, t-shirts, hooded jumpers, etc) to smart clothing (suit, tie, polished shoes, etc).
Results found women always rated the smartly dressed men as more attractive, and significantly so.

When the genders are reversed, men aren't particularly swayed by what women wear. A hot women is a hot women, no matter what she has on. Likewise, unattractive women don't become stunning by dressing up. I believe this is why many men neglect their wardrobe. They wrongly assume women think like men, and aren't influenced by what a person wears. This mindset must change. What you wear is vitally important to a woman's perception of you and how attractive you appear.

## *Update your Wardrobe*

It's difficult to give specific fashion advice in a book. What looks good on you may not look so good on another man, and vice versa. Additionally, fashion is constantly changing. What's *en vogue* this year could become *passé* the next. Luckily for us, men's fashion moves at a glacial pace, and most stylish attire is timeless.

Let's go over some basics. The aforementioned psychological tests show that smart clothing is the way to dress. With this in mind, add the following to your wardrobe.

### Shirts

There are two types of shirt, casual and formal. Formal are the kind worn with a suit and tie. For these, white is best. It goes with everything, no matter what colour/style the rest of your outfit. Alternatively, stick to light pastel shades and avoid bold colours.

If you're in shape, go for a 'slim fit' cut. This will reduce the bagginess of the shirt around your waist and help enhance that 'V' shape torso. If you're carrying extra weight, go for the regular fit; it's looser and more flattering to your midriff.

Casual shirts aren't designed to be worn with a suit and tie. They come in a variety of styles, such as the 'Oxford' and 'Grandad collar' shirt. These are perfect 'smart casual' attire.

There are a few things to avoid with casual shirts: bold colours (except black), arresting patterns, embroideries, logos, and 'Cuban' style collars. Never wear short sleeved shirts: buy long and roll the sleeves up.

Ensure the shirts you wear actually fit you. If you can't do up the top collar button, it's too small. Likewise if the fabric is stretched anywhere, especially around the buttons.

With the top collar button done up, you should be able to comfortably slide a couple of fingers between your neck and the shirt. If you could slide your whole hand down there, the shirt's too large.

Always iron your shirts. Ensure they're wrinkle-free and have creases down the arms, even with casual shirts.

## **Trousers**

As with shirts there are casual and formal styles. It's best to buy your formal trousers as part of a suit. Casual trousers generally don't have matching jackets. Unlike shirts, avoid light coloured trousers - go for darker shades.

Typically, trousers come in two types of fit, 'regular' and 'slim'. The latter are tighter around the legs and are hit or miss in the looks department. Stick with regular fit where you can.

Trouser length is perhaps the first things people notice about them. If they're too long, the fabric bunches up over your shoes. If too short, they ride above your ankles exposing your socks. Both look terrible.

When stood upright, the perfect length would have the trouser barely touching your shoes, just below ankle height. Always wear shoes when trying on new trousers to check for this.
Formal trousers must be ironed with a neat crease on the front and rear. Avoid patterned material and pinstripes - unless you want to look like an 1980s stockbroker.

Casual trousers, or chinos, needn't have a crease, but must still be ironed and wrinkle-free.

## **Suit Jacket/Blazer**

You've guessed it, they come in casual and formal. Formal jackets come as part of a suit, casual versions don't.

Same rules apply for formal jackets as with trousers - dark colours preferably. It's important the jacket fits well; don't go larger because it's comfortable and feels more like a overcoat. When buttoned up, the jacket should fit snug and you should be able to just slide your hand into the jacket via the opening at the chest. If you can fit your whole arm in there, it's too large. Conversely, if it's a squeeze to button up, it's too small.

Arm length is another factor. You want the sleeves of the jacket to end around your wrist when the arms are hanging down by your side. If they're higher than this the arms are too short. If the sleeves are lower and touching your hands, they're too long.

Ideally, with arms hanging by your sides, your shirt sleeve should end where the hand begins, and the jacket sleeve should ride half an inch above that.

You may struggle to find a suit off the rack that fits as I've described. That's perfectly normal - we're all different shapes and sizes. Just buy the next size up and find a tailor to make alterations. It will be well worth the investment.

Casual jackets needn't fit so snug across the torso, but correct sleeve length is still a must. Casual jackets also look good in a variety of colours and patterns, so don't feel constrained to plain dark materials here. Just avoid bold, bright colours and stick to natural tones.

### Footwear

Smart, polished shoes are a must. Leather Oxford or Brogue styles are available in several shades. Black is best, though brown goes well with navy and grey trousers. For a more casual look, boots are the way to go. 'Chelsea' style are versatile and available in leather or suede. Any natural colour looks good: browns, tans or even grey.

### Miscellaneous

You'll want to invest in some jumpers, a coat and a belt or two. Simple wool jumpers work best. Stick to natural colours (i.e. nothing bright or bold) and try 'crew neck', 'v neck' and 'roll neck' styles. Give cardigans a miss.

For coats try a wool overcoat or 'peacoat'. Avoid light colours as they attract stains/marks and look grubby after a few wears.

Belts should match the same colour as the shoes you're wearing. Always leather, never fabric.

## Fashion Faux Pas

Now on to the 'don't wear' list. Generally women find casual gear a turn off. The more 'dressed down' you are, the less attractive you'll appear. With this in mind, avoid the following:

- T shirts
- Hooded jumpers
- Jeans
- Jogging bottoms
- Trainers
- Baseball caps
- Sportswear in general

It's not just what you wear that makes an impact, but how you wear it. Your clothes must be clean, neat/ironed, and fit properly. There's no point owning a great outfit if it looks like you've slept in it. Invest in a full length mirror if you don't have one around the house and check you look good. Shoes polished, shirt tucked into trousers and everything looking new.

## When to 'Dress Up'

Most men will make the effort to dress up for dates. That favourite shirt will come out of the wardrobe and face an ironing. Maybe the uncomfortable shoes will make an appearance too.

But to become a desirable man, this mindset of 'dressing up' only for dates must change. That list of clothing dos and don'ts isn't for date night only. It's for every single day. Each time you leave your house, even if it's only to buy a pint of milk, dress right. Wear a shirt and jacket, put on those trousers and boots.

Initially you may feel awkward and overdressed, but trust me, it will change your life. When you dress smartly, everybody will treat you differently. You will feel respected and noticed. People will comment of your appearance, possibly for the first time in your life. Strangers will point out your nice boots, and ask where you bought your jacket from.

The positive feedback felt from others will fill you with confidence. You'll also feel more comfortable on dates because you're no longer wearing that fancy shirt and shoes; you're just wearing what you always do.

Dress as though at any time you could be magically transported to a date, and you're happy to be suitably dressed for it.

Of course there are exceptions to this dress code. Wearing a uniform for work, appropriate gear for exercising/playing sports, suitable attire for extreme weather etc are a few reasons. But for the most part, any time you're out of your house and people will see you, make the effort and dress right.

### *Personal Experience*

My first foray into the world of fashion happened when a female work colleague offered to take me clothes shopping. Prior to this, I didn't give two hoots what I wore in my own time. T shirts and jeans until they literally fell apart were fine by me. Like most men, clothes shopping was a chore, to be done only when absolutely necessary.

During that first excursion, my friend had me try on trousers that felt way too tight, shirts I'd never consider wearing, and jackets many multiples more expensive than I would usually pay.

I didn't feel comfortable in this new gear. I felt as though I was 'dressing up' for no reason at all. What soon changed my opinion was the reaction from others. Besides a few friends initially teasing me, the response was overwhelmingly positive. People would constantly comment on my clothing, and not just friends or acquaintances. I've been stopped in the street several times by men asking me where I'd bought my jacket, shoes, or whatever.

We really do judge books by their covers - smarten up your wardrobe and discover this for yourself.

# Exercise

Think of an archetypal man, someone who exemplifies masculinity. He could be an actor, sportsman, politician, someone from your personal life, or even a fictional character. Whoever you've thought of, you can guarantee they have one quality in abundance: strength.

That strength could be a psychological trait. The strength to endure and persevere through hard times. To stand up for what they believe in, no matter what personal cost.

That strength could also be physical. Pushing their body to the limits in achieving great deeds. Or having the grit and fortitude to work, day in day out until they've reached a goal.

Strong men are respected, celebrated, and attractive. You must work on become physically fit and strong if you want to be a desirable prospect. This doesn't mean going to extremes and training to become the next Arnold Schwarzenegger. It simply means avoiding the unattractive alternative: a man who is weak and unhealthy.

Losing fat and gaining muscle will increase your appeal to women, even if you do nothing else this book recommends. A slim waist, broad shoulders and big arms are a turn on for almost every woman. They're not only physically attractive features, they also show you're capable of protecting her, and able to provide through work.

Exercise is beneficial in so many ways. Not only will it make you healthier, it will produce endorphins and other hormones that will make you feel great. It will demonstrate discipline and commitment. When playing sports you will meet others and expand your social circle. You will have the chance to learn new skills, become competent and even impressive in some form of activity.

## Where to Start

If you're new to exercise, two factors are most important. Firstly, any exercise is better than none at all. Don't become disheartened because you're initially failing to see results or can't keep up with others. Persevere and expect long term benefits. It's not like buying a new outfit and seeing an immediate payoff.

Secondly, don't be reckless and injure yourself. All physical activities, no matter how seemingly pedestrian, have the potential for harm. Poor technique, not warming up properly, or a gung-ho attitude can cause all sorts of issues, some serious. Don't push yourself too hard until you know what you're doing. Follow the guidance of instructors/those with more experience, and always listen to your body. If it doesn't feel right, stop.

With those pointers in the back of your mind, where to start? If you're already fairly active and exercise/play some sport of other, feel free to skip this section.

Two forms of exercise can be done almost any time, any place and with minimal or no equipment required: walking and calisthenics.

Walking isn't just a way to get from point A to point B, it's fantastic for your health. Regular walks can reduce blood pressure, strengthens bones and joints, increases endurance and can help improve your posture. You don't have to set aside specific time to go for a walk, incorporate it into your daily routine. Take the stairs instead of lifts and escalators. Where possible, walk instead of drive. Most modern phones contain software that tracks your daily walking distance. A common goal is 10,000 steps per day, or around 5 miles. That may be unrealistic due to time constraints, but whatever your current step count, aim to increase it.

Calisthenics is the fancy term for body weight exercises. You'll be familiar with most of them and have probably performed them at some point in your life. Press ups, sit ups, pull ups, squats, jumping jacks, planks, all come under this category.

It's beyond the scope of this book to provide a workout routine (countless books are dedicated to just that), but there is plenty of free, excellent information online. There you can learn which exercises to perform, and how to perform them safely and effectively.

Both walking and calisthenics should be performed daily and form the foundation of your physical training. Beyond these two, take up at least one more activity or sport. Something you can perform regularly and will enjoy.

It could be building on that walking/calisthenics combo by taking up running or weightlifting. If that doesn't take your fancy, perhaps martial arts, cycling, or rock climbing. Otherwise take up a team sport and join your local football, rugby, basketball, or whatever team.

If you don't know what to do, try out several. Most activities have free introductory sessions to see if it's something you wish to pursue.

Whatever you decide, make sure it's physically demanding and fun.

> ### *Personal Experience*
>
> I love weightlifting. Although I lack the genetics and appetite to become really muscular, I thoroughly enjoy this form of exercise.
>
> Despite my enthusiasm for strength training, I can't stand gyms. I've been to many over the years but I've never enjoyed the experience. Queues for the most popular equipment, weight plates strewn about, constant distraction from others - and that's during the quiet periods.
>
> If this sounds familiar, don't let the gym environment put you off from an enjoyable and rewarding form of exercise. With a bit of space at home, you can create your own gym. Initially just a pair of dumbbells will get you started. Over time you could add a foldaway bench, a barbell and some squat stands.
>
> Don't feel you must attend a gym to see results, you can get plenty done without leaving your house. Arguably one of the $20^{th}$ century's finest physiques, Bruce Lee's, was achieved almost entirely from home. He didn't need a gym membership, and neither do you.

# Diet

As with exercise, diet is a subject far too broad and complex to go into detail in this book. But suffice to say what you eat is paramount in gaining muscle and losing fat. It's worth researching this topic in your own time, but here are a few important notes on diet.

### Calories

We eat because food provides us with energy. This energy is measured in units called 'calories'. If a food is high in calories, it means it's energy rich. If we consume more energy than we use, our bodies store that surplus as fat, and we gain weight. If we consume less energy than we use, our bodies will use our fat reserves and we will lose weight.

Every single diet works on this basic principle. If 'energy in' is less than 'energy out', you lose weight. If 'energy in' is greater than 'energy out', you gain weight. Put simply, if you want to lose weight, eat less. If you want to gain weight, eat more.

### Nutrients

If calories are the only factor in gaining or losing weight, is it possible to slim down by eating only chocolate? Absolutely. You could exclusively eat Mars bars for breakfast, lunch and dinner and still lose weight: so long as the total calorie intake is less than the calories you burn each day.
However, a diet consisting only of chocolate would make you incredibly unhealthy. Calories aren't the only factor determining a wholesome diet, there are also 'nutrients'.

Nutrients are the building blocks of food. They include: fats, proteins, carbohydrates, vitamins, minerals and water. Each are essential to the health and wellbeing of our bodies. A chocolate-only diet is high in carbohydrates and fat, but seriously lacking in everything else.

### Basic Pointers

- The consensus from experts is a diet high in protein if you want to build muscle. This means meat, fish, eggs, diary products, soya and beans.

- By all means use protein supplements (shakes, bars etc), but remember these are protein *supplements* not protein *replacements*. The above list of real foods should always be the priority.

- Cut down on carbohydrates. Foods high in carbohydrates include bread, pasta and potatoes. These high-energy foods should be eaten with protein and not in lieu of it.

- Sugar is also a carbohydrate, and incredibly calorific. If you want to be really healthy, cut it out completely. Avoid sweets, desserts, and anything with 'added sugar' in its ingredients.

- Stick to water. No soft drinks, juices or squash/cordials.

Your diet not only determines your weight and appearance, but also your general health. A poor diet can cause fatigue, high blood pressure, impair mental function, tooth decay, cancer, diabetes and a whole host of invisible problems. An unhealthy man is unattractive - fix your diet.

# Physical Appearance

Dressing smartly, becoming fit and strong, and eating a sensible diet will put you lightyears ahead of most other men. But there are a few more considerations before you'll become your most handsome self.

### Grooming

Opinion polls on grooming are full of conflicting results. Women love men with beards, and hate them. Prefer men with short hair, and long hair. Want a shaved chest, and a hairy one... and so on, and so on. There's very little consensus on *how* men should be groomed, except that they *should* be groomed.

No matter what your style, put in the effort and maintain it. Don't let your hair, beard and nails grow unabashed. The hair on your scalp grows approximately half an inch per month, so to keep it looking neat, visit the barber once a fortnight or so. If you have facial hair, keep it tidy and don't neglect to shave your neck and cheeks.

Keeping well groomed shows a woman several positive qualities. You take care of yourself and value your appearance. That you have the means and the time to work on your appearance. It shows discipline, self-respect and conveys status. It's no coincidence society's most well-groomed men are its most successful, and least-groomed are homeless.

As for particular hairstyles and facial hair recommendations, that's entirely up to you. No matter how you look, from 'man-bun' to completely bald, you're never going to appeal to *all* women, so don't bother trying.

Whatever your style, don't fight whatever hand nature's dealt you. If your hair's thinning and you're going bald, cut it short or shave it off entirely. A combover is never an attractive look. Likewise for facial hair. If your beard is wispy and patchy, shave it off and accept defeat. Work with what you have, not what you wish you had.

### *Personal Experience*

I'd always hated haircuts as a child. No matter what the barber did, it never looked right to me. As soon as I'd left school and was no longer bound by a dress code, I grew my hair. I'd kept it around shoulder length and usually styled with an alice band or tied it up in a top-knot. I'm not exaggerating when I say my hair was my pride and joy - my absolute favourite feature. It looked great, and at the time (early 2000s) was uncommon for men to have such long hair, unless they were in a rock band. I was asked constantly by women what my 'secret' was (always towel dry and never use conditioner, if you're interested).

In my early twenties, I'd realised I was thinning on top. Getting out of the shower with wet hair, I could see my scalp. That was the beginning of the end for my luscious locks. A year later and I'd taken the painful decision to shave it all off. Almost twenty years on and I still miss my hair, but it was the right thing to do. If, like me, you're thinning on top, don't fight it. Take the bull by the horns and shave it off. You're in good company.

**Posture**

Our lifestyles are increasingly sedentary. Many of us sit at a screen all day for work. At home we'll entertain ourselves with computer games, Netflix or social media. With online shopping and delivery apps, we needn't leave our homes for essential supplies. This lack of activity takes it toll on our bodies, least of all our posture.

Some postural issues are naturally occurring and are often discovered and fixed in childhood. Others are the result of how we use our bodies daily. A common postural issue linked to sitting all day is slouching. Here the ribcage tilts downwards, moving the neck and head forwards. This gives the 'hunched' appearance, and can remain the default posture even when standing upright.

Over time, the various muscles used to keep us upright can tighten and weaken. To stand upright then takes real conscious effort. There's plenty of great, free information online on how to fix your posture. Research a suitable stretching routine and stick with it. You'll literally become inches taller and appear more confident, looking forwards rather than down at the ground when walking.

## Hygiene

If you've read any dating stories online, you'll be familiar with the typical disasters. Dates looking nothing like their photos or lying about their age happen all too often. But another common theme is hygiene, or lack of it.

Obviously, there are going to be times when you're not smelling your best: immediately after a long day of manual labour, or a session at the gym spring to mind. But it should go without saying, on a date should not be one of those occasions.

Shower or bathe daily. Brush, floss and use mouthwash twice daily. Change overwear and shirts daily. If *you* can smell you, other people definitely can. Roll on deodorants last all day and a little aftershave/cologne goes a long way to making a great first impression.

# Wealth

*"A broke man is like a broke hand. Can't do nothing with it."*

>  Chris Rock
>  stand-up comedian

It gets a laugh from the audience, but comedian Chris Rock makes a serious point when discussing love. As he puts it, unlike women, children and dogs, men aren't loved unconditionally. Being financially solvent is a common string that's attached to a woman's affection.

Obviously, we can't all be rich; most of us never will be. But at a minimum, you've got to be self-sufficient and not rely on others to put food on the table and a roof over your head. Your ideal financial situation can be summed up bluntly - *richer than her*.

Remember hypergamy? Women always prefer to 'marry up', and money is a cornerstone of this concept. To be a desirable prospect, you needn't compete with Elon Musk, you just need to be in a better financial place than your date.

There is one exception to this rule: if a woman sees you're a worthwhile future investment. Take a young, unemployed man who's up to his eyeballs in debt. He's not an attractive prospect for anyone... unless that debt is tuition fees from a recently acquired Oxford law degree.
It doesn't matter so much if you're not earning *now*, so long as there's real potential you'll be earning *later*.

So if you're in a dead-end job with poor career prospects and a stagnant salary, think about some longterm goals. It may be looking at additional training or qualifications. Or maybe pursuing a hobby/extracurricular activity with the view to monetising it at a later stage.

No matter what you're doing now, show that you have a plan and are an attractive longterm investment.

## Interests

What we do with our free time is a better indicator of who we 'really are' than what we do for a living. After all, most of us are obligated to work, and often in jobs we don't want to do. We need money to put food on the table and a roof over our heads. But no one forces you to pursue an interest or hobby, it's something you choose to do.

Women will take note of your leisure activities to help them gauge if you're a suitable partner. The activity itself is irrelevant, it's what it represents that matters. For example, if someone told you they were a keen skier, often played polo, or spent their time sailing yachts. What do you associate with these pastimes? Wealth.
What if they entered triathlons, played in an amateur rugby league, or were competitive weight lifters? Strength and physical prowess.

These interests, and others like them, are most alluring to women: they demonstrate traits desirable in a man. Most men's hobbies aren't so obviously linked to these traits. A keen interest in 1990s indie music, Aztec history, or samurai movies don't demonstrate the qualities women go for.

That's not to say those interests are unappealing, it depends how you spend your time with them. Take art for example. A

man's interest in watercolours could mean two different outlets. Firstly, he may enjoy visiting galleries or even collect paintings. Alternatively, he may be taking art classes and learning to create his own watercolours.
The former is a passive, or consuming type of hobby. He simply watches or collects what he enjoys. The latter is a creative, or participatory type of hobby. He is creating art.

If your current interests or hobbies are passive/consuming, get involved and make them creative/participatory. Love watching football on tv? Join your local team and actually play, or get involved in helping coach a local children's team.

What you do for fun or relaxation says a lot about you; make those pastimes a fascinating part of who you are.

# Happiness

An often overlooked quality, but a vitally important one. You must work on your own happiness and contentment just as you would everything else I've described in this chapter. There is no point being the best dressed, fittest, most accomplished man in the room if you're utterly miserable.

Unfortunately there isn't a universal secret to happiness. It's a completely subjective experience, different for every person. What makes me happy could be hellish for you, and vice versa. Though I feel French novelist George Sand was close to the mark when they wrote: *"There is only one happiness in this life, to love and be loved."*

Many take Sand's 'love' to mean the romantic kind, but I disagree. Reciprocated romantic feelings are hugely significant (it's why you're reading this book), but aren't the only route to happiness. The ancient Greeks believed there were several different types of love besides the romantic.

There is a love felt between friends, between family, a love felt for nature or your fellow man, even a love for yourself.

Each of these should be pursued and cultivated. Putting all your happiness eggs in the romantic basket will lead to disappointment. It may be cliché but if you're not happy by yourself, a woman in your life won't change that. At least not in the long term.

Think about what happiness means to you and what it would take to achieve it more often.

### *Personal Experience*

Richard, an acquaintance of mine, had no luck with women. At least when it came to what he really wanted - a long term relationship. On paper Richard was a catch. He was in his 20s, had a prestigious job, was intelligent, witty and very handsome.

We'd catch up every few months and whenever the topic turned to his love life, he'd pull out his phone and show me pictures of all the women he'd recently met up with. They were all stunning. He had no problem attracting women.

But every connection ended in the same fashion. Things would start off great, he'd take the girl out on a few dates, maybe things would get physical, but after a while they'd always end it. He didn't know why.

It was obvious to everyone except Richard why this kept happening: he was melancholy personified. He was a depressing presence, and would quickly turn any conversation into a complaint or moan. People would roll their eyes when he entered the room. It was his dour attitude that drove women away.

> Richard didn't need to improve his 'game' or become more handsome in order to get dates. He needed to concentrate on himself, work on making his life more enjoyable and become a happier man. Only then would a woman want to be with him for the long run.

## Depression

It would be remiss of me to not mention depression here. According to the charity 'Mind', it's estimated 1 in 6 people in England experience common mental health issues in any given week. Depression is one of the most prevalent.

If you're suffering from depression, it goes without saying my advice to 'be happy' won't cut it. But it's important to note there are different causes of depression:

- Doctors believe there's a genetic component. You're more likely to have depression if others in your family have it too.
- Prescribed medication, alcohol, and recreational drugs can trigger it.
- Your current situation can cause depression. If you've just lost your job or the wife's left you for another man, you're going to be depressed. It's a natural response.

My advice to improve your contentment is aimed more at the latter group. Everything I've suggested in this chapter to become a desirable man will improve your lot and make you happier. Exercising, taking care of your appearance, improving your diet, taking on new interests and hobbies. All of these things will upgrade your current situation and will lift your mood.

If you are depressed and haven't already, seek a medical opinion. Speak to your doctor, or get in touch with a local charity aimed at these things. There's plenty of help out there if you need it - take the first step and reach out for it, you'll be glad you did.

# Confidence

Most men lack confidence when speaking to women they find attractive. It's why we tend to avoid it, unless forced to whilst working, or with some 'Dutch courage' to steady our nerves.

This lack of confidence mostly comes from a fear of rejection and the hurt that comes with it. Imagine yourself at a social event and attempting to strike up a conversation with a man stood next to you. Instead of responding positively, he looks you up and down, pulls a disdained face, and turns his back to you.

You'd probably think to yourself: *"Wow, what's his problem?"* and not give it another moment's thought.

Now imagine an attractive women responding the same way. This time you'd most likely feel upset and embarrassed. It may even ruin your day.

Why do we feel so differently when shunned by women compared to men? It's because we *care* about a woman's opinion of us. The more attractive we find her, the more her opinion matters.

In this scenario, when the woman rejected your attempt to make small talk, it was a personal swipe, an assault on your ego. You were left hurt and belittled.
When the man turned his back on you, it's not taken so personally. He's the one with the problem, not you.

So how can we overcome this fear of rejection and become more confident around women? There are a few methods.

### Fake it 'til you make it

No matter how high your self-esteem, you're not going to feel confident all of the time. The trick is to 'fake it' when feeling nervous or self-conscious. By pretending to be confident and acting as if you are, you'll start to relax and real confidence will set in.

When feeling unsure of yourself, alter your behaviour and try the following:

- Stand/sit upright and look up. When nervous we tend to make ourselves smaller to avoid the attention of others. Change that and make your presence felt. Feel tall and look around you/where you're going.
- Make eye contact. Not just with whomever you're speaking to, but briefly with passersby when they're walking towards you. Avoid the temptation to look down or away from people.
- Relax. Slow down your breathing, lower your shoulders and don't fidget. Make yourself feel as comfortable as possible.
- Slow your speech. When nervous we tend to speak quicker and at a higher pitch. So take your time, articulate your words and deepen your voice.

It won't take long after acting this way, that you'll feel more relaxed and in control of your nerves.

### Experience

It isn't the situation that makes us nervous, but our previous experience of it. When performing anything for the first time where the cost of failure is high, you're going to lack confidence. But after many attempts (both successful and unsuccessful) you'll start to relax and nerves won't get the better of you.

Holding the attention of an attractive woman is exactly the same. The first few times, you'll be nervous as hell, but after a while it'll feel more familiar and routine. Your past experience with women and dating will bolster your confidence.

It may not feel like much consolation now, but understand that your nerves today are paving the way to confidence tomorrow.

## Options

Let's say you've been unemployed for a while. You're running out of savings and after hundreds of applications, you finally get a job interview. No matter how well qualified you are for this role, you're going to be nervous when interviewing for it. Why? Because if you don't get it, it could be months before your next interview. Your lack of options make the risk of failure so much higher.

But what if the job market was more favourable, and your experience/qualifications were in high demand? Then you could interview for several jobs a week, every week. If one application doesn't go well, who cares? You've got several back ups.

Your confidence in this situation is sky high. The risk of failure is minimised by the number of opportunities open to you. The same applies to dating. Working on increasing your options and becoming desirable enough to schedule multiple dates per week does wonders for your confidence in any encounter with women.

## Rationalisation

How would you overcome a fear of spiders? A therapist may suggest two approaches. Firstly, by slowly introducing yourself to your fear. In incremental steps, building up from looking at photos of spiders, to videos, to seeing one at a zoo, to finally holding one for yourself. You can slowly desensitise yourself to the object of fear with increased exposure to it.

Another method is to use rationalisation. To analyse your thought processes and introduce new ideas that may make you think differently, and more positively about spiders. You could learn that the overwhelming majority of spiders are harmless, that they actively avoid humans, that their presence is beneficial for keeping our environments bug-free, that they're more afraid of us than we are of them, etc.

The same process can be used to manage our nerves and improve our confidence around women.

If you've arranged a date with a woman, the following thoughts will help alleviate your nervousness.

- Women have a lot of options and aren't obligated to go on dates. If she's agreed to go out with you, she already thinks you have potential and probably likes you more than you realise.
- She's definitely going to be more nervous than you are. Most of us don't appreciate the risk woman take when meeting a man for the first time. She'll be thinking of her personal safety in a way you'll never have to on dates.
  A worst-case scenario for you is that your date doesn't look like her photos. Her worst-case scenario is being physically assaulted, or worse. So keep things in perspective.
- Besides not looking like her photos, what is the worst that can happen? If she really doesn't like you, or you end up embarrassed, you've still benefitted from the experience.
  You now have another date under your belt, and potentially a humorous story to tell friends in the future. If a date doesn't work out, in a months time it'll make no difference to your life. You'll never see or hear from that person again, and no one in your life will even know the date happened.

## *Personal Experience*

In my early twenties I worked in a busy complaints department for an organisation. I would speak to customers, usually face to face, and attempt to resolve their issues.

A few times per week I'd have to deal with someone who had completely lost their temper. I'd be shouted at, threatened and called every name under the sun.

I'd become so flustered in those situations, I developed a stutter when nerves got the better of me. I'd never stuttered before in my life. With the adrenaline pumping, I could feel my legs turn to jelly and my heart rate increase. I'd feel impotent and weak. Not a pleasant experience.

Initially I thought I wasn't cut out for that kind of work. In the face of confrontation, I felt powerless and literally lost the ability to speak properly.

I stuck at it for a few years, and I'm glad I did. With this constant experience, each irate customer would leave me slightly less flustered. Over time, and with countless arguments under my belt, I became unflappable. No matter how abusive or threatening a customer was, it couldn't unnerve me. I'd dealt with verbal arguments so often, it became water off a duck's back.

With this confidence, I could resolve almost any situation. By maintaining my composure and standing my ground, I became the go-to guy for the worst complainants. A far cry from the trembling, stuttering mess I began the job as.

The point of my story is this: no matter your starting point, you can become competent and confident in almost anything. You just need exposure and practice. Dating/speaking to attractive women is exactly the same, so don't be disheartened when just starting out.

## Chapter Summary

- To become a desirable man you must improve your physical appearance and your ability to provide and protect.

- Women are extremely swayed by what you wear. Changing your wardrobe will effortlessly make you more attractive.

- Ditch casual clothing and dress up 'smart'. Shirts, trousers, shoes, jackets are the way forward.

- Don't just 'dress up' for dates or special occasions. Make smart wear your default outfit. Enjoy the positive attention you'll receive and let it reinforce how important clothing is to other's opinions of you.

- Incorporate fitness and strength training into your daily routine. It needn't be anything elaborate or time consuming. Bodyweight exercises and plenty of walking throughout the day are a great foundation to getting in shape.

- Clean up your diet. Regularly eating calorific, innutritious food will make you physically and mentally ill. Ditch sugar and high carbohydrate foods and increase your protein intake for best results.

- Ensure you're well groomed and presented. Wear clean clothes and shower/bathe every day. Regularly shave/trim your beard and get your hair cut.

- Improve your posture. Learn to stand and walk upright - if you don't know for certain you're doing it, you're probably not.

- Become financially self-sufficient. If you're not currently able to provide food and shelter for yourself, work on doing so. Seek ways of increasing your earning potential, either through qualifications, experience or a change of career.

- Develop at least one creative or participatory interest/hobby. A pastime you can actively pursue and enjoy achievements from.
- If you're not happy by yourself, a woman in your life won't change that in the long term. It's cliché but true. Work on your own contentment, become a happier man.
- Build your confidence/self-esteem. You can do this by 'faking it' and behaving confidently, gaining experience around attractive women, and changing your mindset.

# PART 3

# Online Dating

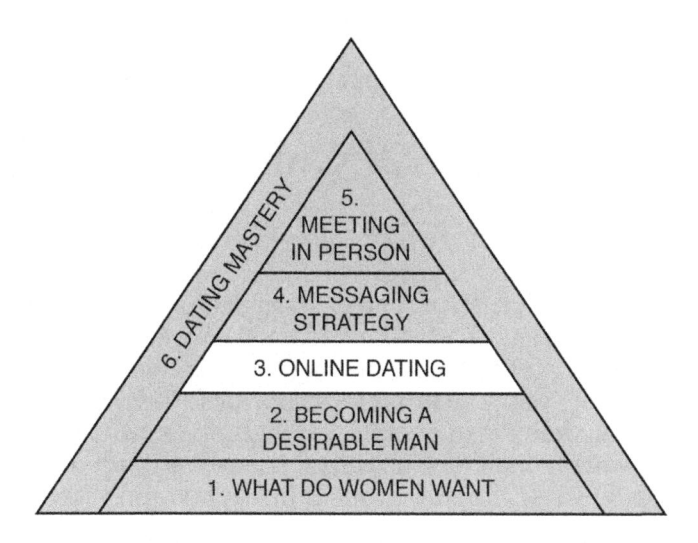

```
              /\
             /  \
            / 5. \
           /MEETING\
          /IN PERSON\
         /------------\
        / 4. MESSAGING \
       /   STRATEGY     \
      /-------------------\
     /   3. ONLINE DATING  \
    /-----------------------\
   /    2. BECOMING A        \
  /      DESIRABLE MAN        \
 /-----------------------------\
/    1. WHAT DO WOMEN WANT      \
---------------------------------
```
(with "6. DATING MASTERY" along the left side)

Previous generations met partners in a few different ways. They were introduced by mutual friends or through family. They attended the same schools or places of work. They also met whilst out socialising. These methods of finding love have been the same since time immemorial.

This all started to change however at the end of the 20$^{th}$ century.

In the 1960s, students at various US colleges including Harvard, Stanford and MIT were creating computer programs to help match singletons. Questionnaires captured personal details and preferences before being fed into a computer. An algorithm then suggested suitable partners from a database. This was the precursor to today's most popular method of finding a partner: 'Online Dating'.

The following chapter will introduce you to online dating and teach you how to create an attractive profile.

# A Brief History Of Online Dating

Prior to the internet, if you'd struggled to find a partner through the usual channels of friends, work, or socialising, there was an alternative. 'Personal ads' have been around for hundreds of years. Through magazines, newspapers and journals, readers could submit a paragraph or two advertising to the world their availability. Interested suiters would respond by letter, hoping to meet in person and take it from there.

The 1990s saw the invention of the World Wide Web, and with it, personal computers and the internet became mainstream. Websites began replacing traditional printed media. No longer would you need to own an encyclopaedia, consult the 'yellow pages', or even buy a newspaper; everything you wanted to read was now available online.

It wasn't long before personal ads were also digitised. One of the first dating websites, Match.com was launched in 1995. It allowed users to create their own profiles, describing themselves and what they were seeking. After paying a subscription, users could read other profiles and send messages to those who caught their eye.

Several other dating sites appeared around this time, all using the same personal ad concept. Some catered to particular demographics: 'JDate' for single Jews, 'Shaadi' for Indian/Pakistani/Bangladeshis looking for marriage, and 'Gaydar' for gay and bisexual men. These websites from the '90s are still in operation today.

By the early 2000s, online dating was responsible for bringing together more couples than meeting through work, education, or friends and family. It was no longer viewed as an odd or embarrassing way of meeting someone. Websites around this time, such as eHarmony and OKCupid went beyond the simple personal ad format. By now users could attach multiple photos of themselves, answer probing questionnaires, and use filters to find exactly the type of person they were looking for.

The modern era of online dating began a decade later with the event of smartphones. By the early 2010s, most of us had handheld devices with built in cameras and access to the internet. Traditional dating websites made way for 'apps', software applications designed to run on mobiles.

As of the 2020s, thanks to apps such as Tinder, Badoo and Bumble, online dating is now far and away the most common way of meeting people and starting relationships. It's estimated almost half of all new relationships are now initiated by online dating.

### *Personal Experience*

My first experience of online dating was in the early 2000s. I'd tried my luck with some of the popular websites of the time, but had no success with them. Almost every aspect was negative. There seemed to be very few women in my area, despite it being London, a city of millions. I didn't receive a single unsolicited message, nor a response to any message I'd sent - my inbox was empty. And the icing on the cake - I was paying a subscription fee for the privilege of all this disappointment and wasted time. Clearly, online dating wasn't working for me.

Realising there must be a better alternative I looked elsewhere and found Gumtree, a classified ads website. Now used mostly to advertise goods for sale, house shares, and tradesmen, it used to have a lively dating section. There, much like the personal ads from days gone by, you had *carte blanche* to write whatever you like and wait for responses.

All posted ads were listed in chronological order, and after a few days they disappeared into the internet ether.

This was the start of my online dating education. Through trial and error, I'd learned what it took to make a successful ad and get responses from interested women, even without the use of photos. It wasn't long before I was able to secure dates, form relationships, and even make lifelong friends.

Although online dating is very different now, those early days of personal ads were a solid foundation for me to build my dating success upon. In the following chapters, I'll be sharing what I've learned and how you too can succeed.

# The Pros And Cons Of Online Dating

To some, online dating is a contentious subject. They may have tried in the past and now hold a robust negative opinion of it. I'm not ignorant to online dating's downsides; I've thoroughly experienced them. But the pros outweigh the cons, and ultimately, it's the best way to meet women and start relationships.

### Positives

Let's start with the pros of online dating and why I'm an advocate of it.

## Online Dating is Ubiquitous

It's estimated over 30% of all adults in the US have used online dating. With similar figures across developed nations, that's hundreds of millions of users worldwide. Online dating is no longer the preserve of basement-dwelling antisocials. It's used by everyone, including the rich, the beautiful and even celebrities; folks you wouldn't assume need help finding a date.

With all these people online looking for love, your pool of potential partners is huge. And this number is increasing year on year. With so many women using it, you'd be foolish not to.

## Limitless Catchment Area

With traditional dating, you're limited to a few square miles in which to find a partner. A woman who works where you do, drinks where you do, or has mutual friends is going to be a local lass. With online dating, the world is your oyster. You can cast your net to the other side of town, country, or even the world if you're so inclined. Where you live, work and play is no longer a roadblock to finding someone special.

## No Ambiguity

Imagine a new woman starting at your place of work. She's attractive and you get on like a house on fire. You'd like to ask her out, but would she be interested? There's no way of knowing until you ask - and that comes with its own risks (see 'Consequence-Free Rejection' below). She may already be in a relationship, you may not be her type, or maybe she's happy being single.

With online dating, there's none of this ambiguity. If she's on a dating app, it's because she's looking for a date. If she's talking to you, it's because she's interested.

## Consequence-Free Rejection

Let's say you pluck up the courage and ask your workmate out for a drink. If she says 'yes' great, but if she says 'no' there could be a few unintended consequences to think about. Best case scenario, it's an embarrassing conversation you both move on from. But chances are you've soured the friendship, making working with her awkward. If other colleagues find out about your failed attempt, it could create rumours affecting your reputation or labelling you a 'creep'.

If you'd totally misread her potential interest in you, it could even result in disciplinary action for unprofessional behaviour.

Being rejected by strangers online is a completely anonymous affair. Yes, it may be upsetting or embarrassing, but no one else will ever know it happened. You won't be ostracised or ridiculed for it.

## Increased Productivity

In 30 minutes, you could initiate a conversation with a dozen or so attractive women online. In the 'real world' this is impossible. Logistically, think of the last social event you'd attended. How many attractive single women were there? How many could you have potentially approached? Not many I assume. Even if there was no ambiguity and you had no fear of rejection, the number of women you could speak to in person pales in comparison to online dating.

Let's be generous and say one in every dozen women find you desirable enough to date. How long would it take you to approach a dozen suitable women in person with the intention of arranging a date? Weeks? Months? Years? Online it would take minutes.

## Preferences

With online dating you can filter out exactly what you're looking for in a partner. This doesn't just mean superficial factors like hair colour and height, etc, but also the important stuff. Are political/religious beliefs (or lack of them) important to you? Are you happy to date a divorcee with children? Are you vegan and looking for the same in a partner? No matter what your dealbreakers are or what's on your wishlist, you can filter for those qualities to help find your perfect match.

## Increased Opportunities

Traditional ways of finding a partner are almost entirely dependant on luck. It doesn't matter how desirable you are as a man if you're too busy to socialise, have no women at work, and your friends/family don't know anyone to pair you up with. Through no fault of your own, you'll remain single.

Online dating broadens your horizons and allows you to take charge of your love life. You don't have to be a victim of circumstance and pin your hopes on the woman of your dreams randomly visiting your favourite bar while you happen to be there.

## *Negatives*

It's not all plain sailing looking for love online. There are a few significant downsides.

## Time and Effort

Online dating's *raison d'être* is to facilitate meeting someone in person. But before you can start arranging dates with women, you'll have to jump through a few hoops. You'll have to send an introductory message that gets a response, engage in some lighthearted back and forth before exchanging numbers, then maybe an in depth text conversation before finally agreeing to meet.

This whole pre-date courtship usually takes a week or two - and at any point could end abruptly, forcing you to start the process all over again.

No matter how great you are at securing dates, your failures will outnumber your successes many times over. You'll send plenty of initial messages before you receive a single response. Most responses won't evolve into conversations. And the majority of conversations won't result in exchanging numbers, and so on.

The 'initial-message-to-first-date' ratio will be hundreds, if not thousands, to one. That can mean a lot of time and effort. If you're not prepared to put in the legwork and manage your expectations, you'll be disappointed.

### Gender Inequality

Although not a walk in the park for either sex, some online dating issues are almost exclusively felt by us men. Like it or not, you will be doing most of the work when it comes to establishing a connection, maintaining a woman's interest, and arranging a date.

Think of this in terms of hunting and fishing. A hunter has to seek out his prey, skilfully pursue it before finally capturing/killing it. A hunter cannot rely on his quarry to come to him: if he wants to eat that night, he has to work for it.

Fishing is different. You don't chase after fish, you use a lure to attract their attention and bring them to you. It's a passive way of achieving the same aim.

When it comes to online dating, women are fishing. They create a profile to attract men. Once their inbox is full of messages, they separate the wheat from the chaff and respond to a small group of men who will compete for her attention.

Like it or not, you're cast in the role of hunter; you'll have to earn those dates. Playing the fisherman online won't work for you unless you happen to be an exceptionally desirable man.

### Emotionally Draining

In most endeavours, the reward you get out is proportional to the effort you put in. Online dating doesn't always play by this rule. If you don't know what you're doing, you could put in hundreds of hours of effort for practically no payoff.

This constant failure to get a response, to get a conversation going, to arrange dates can take its toll on your mental health. Even the most resilient of us can only take so much rejection before cutting our losses and calling it a day.

It's no fun feeling like you're wasting your time, and it's less fun feeling ignored and undesirable.

### Male to Female Ratio

On Tinder it's estimated there's something like four men for every woman using the app. Those aren't great odds, especially considering women outnumber men in most general populations.

This means competition is fierce, where literally thousands of men can be competing for the same attractive woman. Going back to our hunter analogy, it's hard enough to catch prey in isolation; it's exponentially harder when you're not the only hunter.

A woman's 'fisherman' dating strategy, combined with the disproportionate amount of men, means her inbox is overwhelming, and it's increasing every day. Even if you tick all her boxes and are her Dream Guy, she may not even see you've shown interest and doesn't know you exist.

### Pay to Win

Most popular dating sites/apps are free to use, but you're limited to a basic version of their platform. For women this doesn't matter so much. With a 'fishing' strategy, so long as you can create a profile and receive likes/messages, you're good to go.

However, this basic version limits how proactive you can be when looking for a partner. There may be restrictions on: liking profiles, sending messages, filtering search criteria, inbox size, and a whole host of other tools that make your experience so much easier.

In order to give yourself the greatest chance of success and not handicap yourself, you're forced to bite the bullet and open your wallet.

## Disingenuous Profiles

It isn't just children who need to learn 'stranger danger'. Even as a grown man you must exercise caution when speaking to someone you don't know online. Most dishonesty you'll come across is on the harmless side: profile photos from yesteryear, embellishing an exciting social life, etc.

However, there are genuine con artists out there looking to exploit you. This ranges from begging for money for some fabricated emergency, to asking for compromising pictures with an aim to blackmail you after.

Besides outright criminality, which is thankfully rare, there are also women using online dating for the wrong reasons. You'll find: sex workers advertising their services, wannabe 'influencers' looking for Instagram followers, and women who have no interest in dating but enjoy male attention.

## Overchoice

In days gone by, your pool of potential partners was mostly limited by geography. If you weren't in someone's physical presence, you could never start a relationship with them.

Now that isn't the case, and the number of suitable women you could date has increased from dozens to thousands. But is all this choice a good thing?

Studies have shown where there are too many options available, it has a detrimental affect on our decision-making and contentment with the choices we make.

Online dating is a prime example of this. Thanks to the seemingly endless lineup of potential partners, it can seem difficult to feel happy or content with someone if in the back of your mind is the thought... *"maybe I could do better"*.

Was this list of cons enough to put you off online dating? Or maybe it reminded you why you didn't enjoy it in the past.
Don't be disheartened. There are practical ways and thought processes to mitigate those downsides. We'll be exploring them shortly.

## Which Platforms Are Right For You?

There is no *best* dating platform. They're all different in their own way, and given your location, lifestyle, preferences, age, and so on, you're going to fare better on some dating sites/apps than others. But it's difficult to recommend which is right for you via a book. After all, we're all individuals with different circumstances. Platforms that yield great results for me, may not for you and vice versa. Additionally, you may be reading this years after publication, making any specific advice potentially outdated.

So here's some guidance on how *you* can find the best dating platform for yourself.

Firstly, trial and error. You can do your homework on each platform and then decide what's best, but there's nothing like firsthand experience. Try as many platforms as you can. Create profiles and get to work, see how successful you are with each. The acid test is simple: how much interest are you getting? How many responses do you receive to your 'likes' and messages? Go where you're most popular.

What are you looking for? Think about your target demographic and the platform they're most likely using. If you're after a devout Catholic for marriage, Tinder's probably not your thing. Want a short-term, no strings relationship? It's doubtful you'll find it on Christian Connection.

There are platforms that cater to specific preferences, like religious denominations, sexualities, ethnicities, even socioeconomic groups. Whatever you're looking for in a relationship, there's probably a dedicated site/app for it.

Most popular platforms aren't aimed at any particular group but tend to attract a certain type of person anyway. Match, Tinder and OKCupid are open to all, but the kind of woman you'll typically find on each is quite different. Try them all and see which you prefer.

The difference between dating websites and mobile apps isn't just cosmetic. Websites tend to be more text-orientated. This means you'll be doing a bit more reading and writing when it comes to creating a profile and reading others. This also correlates with the type of person using each platform, and their preferred style of communication. If you enjoy lengthier conversations prior to meeting, websites are generally the way forward. If paragraphs of text put you off, stick with the apps.

Don't spread yourself too thinly. By all means try out as many platforms as possible, but once you've found a couple of favourites, stick with those and ditch the rest. Constantly flicking between dozens of platforms, and potentially paying for them, is unnecessary. You'll be wasting your time and effort otherwise.

## *Personal Experience*

My own preference is for dating websites over mobile apps, for a few reasons.

- I'm not show-stoppingly handsome, so I'm much more likely to attract attention with a well-written profile over a single photo.
- Intelligent women are my cup of tea, and in my experience, there's a higher percentage of them on the websites compared to apps.
- Generally, websites attract women more serious about going on dates and finding a partner. There are fewer women on the websites using the platform as an entertaining pastime, or looking to advertise their social media accounts.
- Time management. It's easier to create a routine where you log into the website at certain times and limit your usage. The mobile apps are more like games, designed to be addictive and used constantly throughout the day. This can lead to increased frustration and burnout.

This isn't to say I don't use mobile apps, or you shouldn't - but despite their popularity, they're not my favourite method of online dating.

## Creating A Great Profile

Unless you're a PR consultant or professional resumé editor, it can be a struggle selling yourself to others. Advertising how wonderful you are to the world is an imposing task and most avoid it. Where do you even start, and how do you not come across as a braggart singing their own praises?

Unfortunately, the social rules of 'real life' don't translate well to online dating. Most of us are humble and would only bring up our accomplishments/interesting facts if they came up naturally in conversation. We're happy for others to take their time in getting to know us.

When viewing your dating profile, there is no conversation and there is no time. A woman is going to scan through your pics and skim-read your profile before making a snap decision: *'Is this man desirable?'*

If something caught her eye, she'll take a closer look before confirming you're worth chatting to. This whole process takes seconds.

It's vitally important your dating profile is attractive and instantly shows a woman your strengths and potential as a partner. You can't wait until you get chatting until she learns what a great catch you are, because if she's not interested immediately, it's never going to happen.

The following advice will ensure your profile gets the recognition you deserve.

# A Picture Paints A Thousand Words

There's no avoiding it; you *have* to include photos of yourself, and they *have* to be good to get the most out of online dating. Unfortunately, we as men are disadvantaged when it comes to pictures. Unlike many women, we don't often dress up for outings and document it on social media. You probably don't have dozens of recent photos of you on Instagram to draw from. Most men go years between their picture being taken, and on those odd occasions you may not look your best.

So if you don't already have decent photos of yourself to hand, you'll have to get snapping. Here are a few dos and don'ts for dating profile pictures.

- They have to be recent. There's no point using your favourite pics from a decade ago when you clearly don't look like that any more. You'll be caught out eventually when you meet in person and you've instantly jeopardised the date.

- Studies have shown picture quality has an effect on how attractive you appear. It may be tempting to post a low-res pic to blur those imperfections, but don't. The higher the resolution, the better.

- You'll need three to five photos for your profile. By only posting one or two, it's difficult to gauge what you really look like and this can put off potential matches. Any more than five is unnecessary.

- Include at least one clear photo of your face, unobscured by sunglasses, the environment or an odd camera angle. Also include at least one full body photo, showing what you look like from head to toe.

- Dress smartly and look your best. See previous chapter on what kind of outfits women find most attractive on men and dress accordingly.

- Only use selfies as a last resort, and then make sure the background's interesting. Don't take a pic in the bathroom mirror and expect women to swoon.

- Shirtless posing: just don't do it. Unless you're at the beach in your swimming shorts, or a professional bodybuilder at a competition, keep your top on.

- Be cautious with group photos. On one hand they're great; they show you're sociable and accepted as part of a group, but they can raise a few issues. The most obvious is - which one are you? Not everyone will be able to pick you out from a crowd, especially if you and your friends look similar.
  Additionally, you're going to be compared to the others in your photo. If you're not the tallest, most handsome man in that picture, don't use it. A simple way to solve both those issues is using a photo editor to cover up/blur everyone's faces except yours.

- Avoid photos with attractive women. It may come across as a cheap ploy to infer social status, or gives the impression there are hot women in your life and potential partners have competition. As with group photos, obscure their faces or crop them out entirely.

- Candid photos are best, where you're behaving naturally and the picture's taken without you realising/posing for it.

- Use photos to display traits women find attractive. These include indicators of wealth, status, confidence, strength, etc. So think: picture of you giving the best man's speech at a wedding (status and confidence); picture of you playing a sport (strength and fitness); picture of you abroad on holiday (wealth). Photos aren't just to show your physical appearance, but also your desirability as a man and a potential partner.

- Avoid clichés or unoriginal set ups. You may not realise, but your photos could be almost identical to hundreds of others local to you. Dating pics of men proudly holding up their 'catch of the day' whilst fishing have become so ubiquitous there are news articles deriding it. Stand out from the crowd with photos uniquely you.

Armed with your photos, it's now time to put on your creative hat and get writing.

## Writing Your Profile

Writing a CV/resumé is a straightforward affair. Besides a brief professional summary (*"Experienced and self-motivated team player with a strong track record of delivering... yada yada yada"*), the whole document is a dry list of facts and figures. Where you've previous worked, what your roles entailed, how well you did at school, etc etc.

This format makes it easier for employers to find suitable staff, and for you to showcase your credentials. You're not graded on creative writing skills or ability to captivate the reader; the plain ol' statistics speak for themselves.

Dating profiles are a different kettle of fish. Here you're judged on the delivery, not just the content.
In other words, *how* you describe yourself is just as important as what you're describing. And unlike CVs, there's no standardised format to follow. You're given an empty text box to populate however you see fit.

Due to the success of Tinder, the majority of dating platforms have ditched the need for lengthy essays. Most profiles are now only a paragraph or so long, if that. You may think this makes your job more difficult. After all, how can you accurately describe yourself in just a few lines? The answer is

## Online Dating

you can't - but you don't have to. Dating profiles are like the 'blurb' on the back of a book cover; a brief description to get you interested in making the purchase. It doesn't chronicle the book's plot from beginning to end nor does it list all the characters involved. Its purpose is to grab your attention and get you invested in continuing to read.

A successful dating profile is *anything* that gets a woman's attention and makes her think: *"I want to speak to this guy"*. It could be a single line joke or a 1000 word dissertation. There is no right or wrong format, but there is certainly right and wrong content.

Follow these pointers to ensure your profile gets her attention.

- Nothing kills attraction like negativity. Do not use your profile to air grievances about online dating, complain about your circumstances, or elicit sympathy. If you're struggling to find a match, or you hate your job, or your pet rabbit just died, confide in a friend. Don't share it with potential dates online.

- Show, don't tell. Instead of writing: "I'm intelligent/humorous/wealthy", use your profile to display those attributes. Write an intelligent/humorous profile, or share pictures from your private yacht in Saint-Tropez. Let women see for themselves what you're like, rather than telling them outright. Otherwise you'll be met with skepticism or thought of as a braggart.

- Specific beats generic. Instead of: "In my free time I like to play rugby", try: "Last week I scored five tries in our local derby rugby match - I'm happy to sign autographs." The former is a boring factoid, the latter tells an engaging story.

- Be careful with humour. The above joke works because it's an obvious delusion of grandeur where women can play along (*"Will I get rich selling your autograph on eBay?"*). But some jokes don't translate well through text. What's written for comedic effect may be misconstrued and taken literally. If you're a metalhead but joke about loving some lame manufactured boyband, the irony may be lost and you're taken on your word.

- The above applies doubly for self-deprecation. Never belittle or knock yourself. It may be done in a lighthearted, ironic way but it could be taken at face value. Joking about always missing the bus and being late for work could translate to "I'm unreliable and disorganised" - not attractive traits.

- Try including a 'call to action': a question or statement used to encourage potential dates to get in touch. Make it engaging and specific. Instead of signing off with a boring: "If you think we'd get on, say hello", try something like: "I've just returned from a hiking trip in Peru and already thinking about my next adventure - any suggestions?"

- Don't make a shopping list of what you're looking for in a person or relationship. In fact, don't mention your wants at all. You may come across as arrogant or entitled. Save this for a conversation later. It makes for an interesting talking point once you've exchanged numbers.

- Don't pander, be honest. When describing yourself, especially likes and dislikes, don't include something just because it's popular, or you think it's what women want to hear. Every other guy is doing the same and your profile will be as boring and unremarkable as theirs.

- Minimalist profiles. A single witty observation or joke can work just as well as a full profile. If you're going down this route, either by choice or your preferred app restricts profile length, bear a few things in mind. Your photos will be doing all the heavy lifting - they have to convey your desirable attributes. Ensure your pics are varied, in different settings and activities. Secondly, be original with your one-liner. If it's something hilarious you've just seen on Twitter, everyone's going to be using it. She may skip past your profile if it's the fifth time today she's read 'your' joke.

- *"I enjoy travelling"*, *"Looking for my partner in crime"*, *"I love to laugh"*, *"I'm down to earth/easy going"*. It won't take long before you recognise the same phrases crop up time and time again in dating profile. Avoid these clichés so your summary doesn't read like everyone else's.

Don't stress over crafting the perfect profile. If you follow the above advice, yours will stand head and shoulders above most of the competition. Think of it as a work in progress. The women you speak to will unwittingly give feedback on what works and what doesn't. If everyone's asking about your pet dog, keep that part of your profile. If they're all ignoring your call to action on the best local coffee shops, take it out and try something else.

Remember, the profile is a means to an end - showing you're worth talking to.

## Chapter Summary

- Since its inception in the 1990s, online dating has grown to become the most common way couples meet and begin relationships. It's estimated almost half of all new relationships are currently initiated by online dating.

- There are plenty of pros and cons to this method of finding love. The positives include: lots of people to choose from, you can search the entire globe, rejection is stress-free compared to 'real life', and you can set specific search criteria.

- The downsides to online dating include: it can take a lot of time and effort to establish a worthwhile connection, there's lots of competition from other men, and the constant failure can be emotionally draining.

- There are dozens of online dating platforms to choose from. Trial several and see where you're most successful before committing to one or two.

- Your dating profile will be judged by women in a matter of seconds, if not quicker. You must be able to sell yourself effectively and immediately.

- Posting three to five quality photos is integral to showcasing your desirability.

- Your profile's text isn't necessarily there to inform, but to generate interest. The aim is to grab attention and cast yourself in a positive light, no matter what you write to achieve that.

- Profiles aren't set in stone - regularly update and adapt yours according to how well received your description/photos are.

# PART 4

# Messaging Strategy

# Messaging Strategy

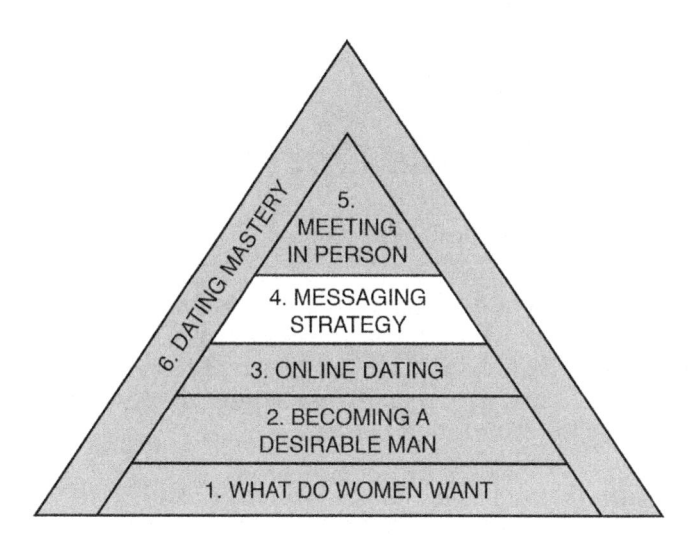

```
              /\
             /  \
            / 5. \
           /MEET- \
          / ING IN \
         / PERSON   \
        /------------\
       / 4. MESSAGING \
      /   STRATEGY     \
     /------------------\
    /  3. ONLINE DATING  \
   /----------------------\
  /     2. BECOMING A      \
 /       DESIRABLE MAN      \
/----------------------------\
/   1. WHAT DO WOMEN WANT     \
--------------------------------
```
*(Pyramid diagram: levels 1–5 inside, with "6. DATING MASTERY" running along the left edge.)*

Once your dating profile is complete and uploaded for the world to see, what's next? Sit back and wait for your inbox to fill with thousands of hot women desperate to date you? I have bad news if that's what you're expecting. This is where the real work starts, and trust me, at times it will feel like work.

As I've mentioned previously, you will have to put in the effort and initiate contact with women. They will not be messaging you. Their 'fishing' strategy doesn't allow time to filter through all the messages they receive and also make a concerted effort to send their own.

Making first contact and starting conversations with women online is something almost all men get wrong. It leads to so much wasted time and effort, and ultimately disappointment. I'm going to show you how to get it right and guide you through capturing a woman's attention, getting a conversation going, and finally arranging dates.

# The Five Terrible Opening Gambits

You can mess up a first move in chess and still recover to win the game. But if your initial message on a dating app isn't good enough, you instantly lose. She won't respond. On the off chance she does, it's usually out of politeness to quickly confirm her low opinion of you.

There are five terrible tactics when it comes to opening messages. Women's inboxes are full of these hopeless introductions. You may have tried a few yourself before realising they don't work.

### 1 - "Hi"

Brevity may be the soul of wit according to Shakespeare, but single-word openers will get you nowhere online. They are the height of laziness. Women are so sick of receiving constant 'Hi', 'Hello' and 'Hey's that many make it clear in their profiles not to send them. So take their advice and don't do it. It gives the impression you have nothing interesting to say, or you're simply spamming every woman online with the same boring opener.

### 2 - Copy/Paste

*"How much does a polar bear weight? Enough to break the ice."* A charming opener, the first 20 times you hear it. It's hard to appreciate how much attention women receive online. It doesn't take long before they've heard every joke/generic opener you can think of. Yes, it's marginally better than a boring 'hello', but it still reeks of laziness. It's no secret you're sending that same copy/pasted opener to every women who takes your fancy. It won't work.

### 3 - The Essay

The above tactics are low effort attempts to play the numbers game. Hoping if you spam enough women one of them will reply. After realising this doesn't work, a few men swing the effort pendulum the other way. They'll carefully peruse a woman's profile before writing a lengthy personalised message. They'll introduce themselves, acknowledge what's in her profile, highlight their similarities, explain why he's a good match, and ask several questions.

This tactic seldom works. Reading and responding to a long introduction with multiple threads and questions takes effort. She's not going to spend that effort on a complete stranger until she thinks you're worth it.

### 4 - Compliments/Sexual Comments

Giving compliments is an effective way to show we appreciate or like someone. And in doing so the recipient is more inclined to appreciate or like us back. But there are important caveats that determine how compliments are received.

- Repetition. If someone complimented your shirt it would make your day. But what if every person you met, day in day out, did the same thing. You'd soon become blasé and that constant flattery will lose its impact.
- Perceived sincerity. People are usually nice to you when they want something in return, and compliments are an easy way to do this. Is the person complimenting being genuine, or is there an ulterior motive behind their kind words? If you suspect the latter, the compliment isn't worth much.
- Bearer's status. It isn't just the compliment itself that matters, but also who's giving it. Compliments mean so much more from someone you like, respect, or even admire. But when it's from a person whom you have no interest in, or even dislike, the compliment has little weight.

Compliments women receive online fall flat because all above caveats apply. They're constantly told how beautiful they are, they know men are only trying to get their attention, and most of the men complimenting are undesirable.

Messages of a sexual nature fare just as poorly as compliments and for similar reasons. A woman must feel attraction and comfort before she's responsive to 'adult' material. That feeling is seldom there from first contact, and may not be established until after meeting in person. Save the blue talk for much later, preferably after she initiates it.

## 5 - Angry/Abusive

These kinds of messages are usually sent out of desperation for a reply. After trying the above tactics with no success, some men don't know where else to turn and get angry or abusive. Complaining that all women are the same and you don't deserve to be ignored, or name-calling/threatening violence won't make women attracted to you. But for some men it's the only way they get a response - even if it's a negative one calling out their behaviour.

It should go without saying, but don't resort to this. The previous openers are forgivable; I've certainly used most of them in the past because I didn't know any better - but there's no excuse for angry or abusive messages. They won't work, they'll get you banned from the dating platform, and you may be guilty of a criminal offence.

Do any of those opening gambits look familiar? If you've used online dating before, I'm certain you've tried some yourself - and with little success.
So if none of those methods work, what does?

## Impactful Openers

An introductory message has one job: to grab the recipient's attention. That's easier said than done, especially if her inbox is as busy as Piccadilly Circus. To stand out from the crowd and give yourself the best possible chance for making a connection, your message must comprise the following:

- It must be bespoke, relating to something in her profile. This shows you've taken time to actually read her summary and comment on it, rather than spam her with some low-effort generic opener you send everyone.
- It must be short; something she can read and digest in seconds. The longer the message, the less likely she is to reply.
- Nothing so obvious that every other man will be sending the exact same comment/question.
- It mustn't be boring or serious. Asking a woman how long she's worked in her current job or how she's coping after the loss of a pet rabbit will not interest her.

Sounds like a challenge? It may not come naturally to start, but with practice you'll soon be composing excellent messages in seconds.

Here's how to create an opener that gets a woman's attention and dramatically improves your odds of starting a conversation.

- Read through her profile and make a mental note of the 'hooks' - the interesting snippets of information that make her unique. Some profiles will be full of them, others may contain only one or two.

Messaging Strategy

- Pick a 'hook' and think of a lighthearted comment or non-serious question relating to it. Don't overthink it, usually the first thing that springs to mind is best.
- If her written summary contains nothing of interest (a common issue), take a look through the pictures and see if there's anything there that catches your attention. Her performing some kind of activity for example. There's your 'hook', think of a comment or question from that.
- If there is absolutely nothing interesting about a woman's profile (in my experience you'll find this in around one in twenty), just move on. It doesn't matter how attractive she is, don't waste your time thinking of something to say.
- Jot down your lighthearted comment/non-serious question. It should only be a sentence long, two at a push.
- Before sending, check for correct spelling and grammar. Refrain from emojis and exclamation marks.
- Send and move on to the next profile.

This whole process, from first reading a profile to sending a message should only take a couple of minutes. When starting out it may take a little longer, but don't get stuck on a profile for more than 5/10 minutes. If you're stuck for something to say, make a mental note of her hooks and move on to another profile. A while later, perhaps the following day, an inspired comment/question may spring to mind.

*Examples*

If that all sounds a bit vague, here are a few demonstrations. Below are 'hooks' taken verbatim from various women's profiles and corresponding example openers. This should give you an idea as to what makes an impactful opener.

# Messaging Strategy

***Hook:*** "I'm halfway to becoming a doctor..."
***Opener:*** "So you can diagnose illnesses but not fix them?"

***Hook:*** "German biologist, new to London..."
***Opener:*** "Is German biology different from the regular kind?"

***Hook:*** "Moved to the UK for a PhD..."
***Opener:*** "Do they hand them out at Heathrow, or did you have to study for it?"

***Hook:*** "Don't give up on your dreams..."
***Opener:*** "I couldn't agree more. It's why I struggle to wake up in the morning."

***Hook:*** "I've probably been to the British Museum once a year since I was born."
***Opener:*** "Aren't you tempted to go every day for a week and then take the next seven years off?"

***Hook:*** "I cook better than your microwave."
***Opener:*** "Maybe, but can you make the 'ping' sound when you've finished?"

***Hook:*** "Looking for a committed relationship, not just a 'partner in crime'."
***Opener:*** "That's a shame. My heist needs a getaway driver and we thought you'd fit the bill."

***Hook:*** "I'm always smiling and laughing..."
***Opener:*** "Even on the train to work? Doesn't that worry other commuters?"

***Hook:*** "I recently spent a month in Madrid!"
***Opener:*** "Was this by choice, or did you get really lost finding the airport on the way home?"

***Hook:*** "I work with primary school children..."
***Opener:*** "Where? What kind of business employs primary school kids??"

***Hook:*** "I'm looking for a male version of me..."
***Opener:*** "Have you tried a fake moustache and mirror?"

***Hook:*** "No gym guys, thanks!"
***Opener:*** "What about Jim guys? It's not my name, but I figured I'd ask anyway."

***Hook:*** "If you're looking for a quick hookup, I have to disappoint you!"
***Opener:*** "How about a slow hookup? We can still disappoint each other, but take our time over it."

***Hook:*** "I don't like vanilla ice cream... I hope you know what I mean ;)"
***Opener:*** "I hear you loud and clear. Lactose intolerance is no joke."

***Hook:*** "Anything you want to know just ask!"
***Opener:*** "Why do planes use those weird double headphone jacks?"

Will any of these openers make their recipient weak at the knees after reading? Absolutely not, but that's not the point. They're attention grabbing. They're daft, playful jokes mostly built on deliberate misunderstanding. They're easy to read and, most crucially, easy to respond to. If she likes you and has a sense of humour, she'll respond by playing along with your daft opener. Without too much effort, you've made a connection and created your first private joke together.

This kind of opener won't necessarily give off 'desirable man' vibes by itself, but it will prompt her to look at your profile. It's then, after reading your summary and looking at your pictures, she'll decide to respond. This two-pronged approach dramatically improves your chances of success: a desirable profile plus an impactful opener.

But even with this proven approach, you'll have to manage your expectations. The majority of messages you send won't garner a reply. No matter what tactics you use, online dating a still a numbers game. But with impactful openers like these, the odds are so much more in your favour. Instead of a response rate in the one per hundreds, you can bring it down to one per dozen.

This is another reason to keep these openers short and sweet. It's as much for your benefit as it is hers. If you want to setup multiple dates per month, or preferably per week, you need to be sending a lot of messages. If they take too much time or effort to write, you'll be handicapping your progress.

# How To Succeed With Impactful Openers

For many, initiating contact is the worst part of online dating. If you're not getting responses, it can be a demoralising chore. But even with a great profile and impactful openers, you're still going to face a lot of rejection. For this reason, creating and sending openers has to be an enjoyable experience. The best way to do this is to treat it like a game.

We measure our success online by the number of replies we receive, conversations we maintain, and dates we arrange. But none of those feats are entirely within our control. There are numerous reasons why your opener may not get a response, many of which have nothing to do with you.

By defining success on events outside our control, and basing our sense of achievement and happiness on those events, we're setting ourselves up for failure and disappointment.

Instead, we must divert our attention to goals entirely within our grasp. We can do this by creating games where the goals are achievable by our actions alone. Timing yourself whilst sending openers is a great example. How many messages can

## Messaging Strategy

you send in 30 minutes? Or how quickly can you create five? By pivoting our mindset from *'will this message get a response?'* to *'how quickly can I create this message?'* you're taking charge of the outcome. Success and the enjoyment from it are now on your terms, not dependant on an outside agency.

Besides timed trials, why not aim for the shortest impactful opener possible? Or a more subjective goal of funniest/daftest opener? Anything that distracts you from thinking solely of getting replies will keep you more engaged and ironically more likely to get responses.

*When* you send openers and to whom also affect your success. It's my experience women are more responsive to your first message if they happen to be online when they receive it. Some dating sites allow you to filter by who's currently/most recently online. Where able, always prioritise this criteria. There are diminished returns when sending openers to women seldom online. If your recipient's only logging in once per week, your opener may be hiding amongst hundreds of others when she next checks her inbox.

Although we're moving towards a 24/7 business culture, where working shifts, nights, and weekends are no longer out of the ordinary, most still work 'office hours'. For this reason there are fewer women online weekdays between 9am-5pm. With experience you'll soon learn which periods are quieter and not worth logging on in your area.

We all have preferences as to what we want in a partner, but to bastardise JFK's inaugural address: *"Ask not who are you attracted to - ask who's attracted to you."* You may have a penchant for tall brunettes, but if it's only short blondes responding to your openers that's where your success lies. Given your age, job, looks, and every other descriptor about you, you're going to be more desirable to certain types of women over others. It makes sense to play to your crowd if you want to get the most from online dating.

I'm not suggesting you should have *no* preferences and just 'get what you're given' - it's important to have dealbreakers. If you really don't want a partner who smokes, is religious, has pets, or whatever, stick to your guns. But don't make the list so exhaustive that you're holding out for some perfect woman who ticks all your boxes. She doesn't exist.

Don't immediately write off a potential match because it's not *exactly* what you're after. Send an opener anyway. It's difficult to accurately judge a person based on their dating profile alone. Worst case scenario, you meet after a week or so of chatting and don't get on. You've still gained from the experience; every conversation you have/date you attend makes you better at it.

Although even modest success requires a lot of sent openers, don't become a slave to the dating app. Set boundaries and limit the time you spend flicking through profiles and writing messages. Many men have a miserable time online and quit soon after joining because they don't pace themselves. To find the love of your life may take a thousand openers, a hundred conversations and dozens of dates. You're not going to squeeze that into a week.

If you go too hard too quickly, you're going to suffer messaging fatigue. If you have no current conversations going, and are purely sending openers, don't spend more than an hour a day on the sites/apps. In addition, take at least one day off a week from it. Online dating's a marathon, not a sprint. Avoid burning out and ensure you can last the long haul - it'll be worth it.

### *Personal Experience*

My daily routine for sending openers has changed considerably over the years. Initially I went at it all guns blazing - logging in frequently, firing off messages morning, noon and night. Like most men, I instinctively knew it was a numbers game: the more messages I sent, the more likely I'd get a reply. It didn't take long to realise this was a fast track ticket to burnout. My mental health would suffer and I'd quit online dating until I'd mustered up enough resilience to try again a month or two later.

Moderation is the key to longterm success. Now I won't spend more than four hours per week sending openers. This time is spread out over four or five days. Usually, long before I reach that four hour mark, I'd have received enough responses and begun a few conversations to stop sending openers entirely.

My preferred time for sending openers is around 9/10pm. By this point I'm finished with work/hobbies/chores and have settled down for the evening. I'll set myself a time trial of say 30 minutes and concentrate solidly on sending openers during that time. After a short break, I'll set another time trial. Usually, before my timer's up, I've managed to get a response and start a conversation.

To keep things interesting, I'll use available filters when sending out openers. By specifying the type of woman I'm looking for, I'll only send messages to blondes on one day, then pet owners the next, then women under 5ft5 the day after, and so on. Over time I'll cycle through all the different options.

My reply rate varies day to day. On a good day, it's something like one response for every six openers sent.

> On a poor day, it's closer to one in thirty, or more. Of course, not every response leads to a proper conversation - something we'll look at in the next section.
>
> My mindset now when sending openers is to prioritise making it fun for myself, and accept that most messages I send won't garner a response.

## Introduction To Conversations

Getting a decent conversation going can be the trickiest part of messaging strategy. Unlike sending openers, or actually arranging a date, the conversation in-between has so many unknown variables. It's impossible to plan out in detail what to say and how to say it beforehand. That said, you won't have to wing it. There's plenty you can learn to ensure your conversations go smoothly.

Before we look at a few pointers, why do we bother with conversations in the first place? Why not cut to the chase and suggest meeting once she responds to your opener? Because unless she thinks you're incredibly desirable, chances are she'll say 'no'. You've then wasted the opportunity and she'll move on to the next guy - who isn't giving off impatient/desperate vibes.

If the opener's job is to get her attention, the conversation that follows gives you time to complete a few more tasks. Namely demonstrate your desirability and build attraction, so when you do ask to meet in person she'll enthusiastically agree. It also gives you time to decide if this is someone you really want to go on a date with. You may discover things about her contrary to your first impression. Maybe a little dishonesty/omission in her profile (e.g. children not previously mentioned, or she isn't technically single), or after a bit of back and forth you realise you're not compatible in some way. Remember it's a two-way process: she'll be sizing you up to see if you tick her boxes, and you should be doing the same with her.

When a conversation goes well, it also takes enormous pressure off the date itself. If you've been chatting for a while, you've already built the beginnings of a relationship. You'll know more about each other, have a few private jokes, and she may let slip she likes you. All bonuses when meeting for the first time.

Occasionally you'll connect with women who have no interest in conversing. They'll respond to your opener, like the look of your profile and ask if you fancy meeting within a couple of messages. When that's the case, and if you're happy to expedite the process, arrange a date and take it from there.

Before you agree to meet, establish the lack of dialogue is due to something reasonable or innocuous. For example, she may work a 70 hour week and simply not have time for a meaningful conversation, or perhaps English is her second language and finds reading/writing laborious.

A lack of conversation prior to meeting may be a red flag. There's an increased chance of getting stood up due to lack of investment, or she may be a serial dater more interested in a free meal/drinks than you.

## The Queue

Before going over conversational dos and don'ts, I'm going to share with you a concept that will help you understand women's behaviour when it comes to dating. It's applicable at every stage of the dating game, from first contact, right up to

## Messaging Strategy

establishing a monogamous relationship, but you'll begin to notice it during the conversation stage. If at any point during courtship you're confused by a woman's actions, this concept may help explain them.

It's something I call 'The Queue'. It's simple to understand and will save you from plenty of uncertainty and potential frustration.

The concept works like so. Imagine every woman you speak to online has a queue of men lining up for her attention. Only this queue doesn't work on the usual basis of 'first come, first served'. The woman is in charge of who stands where. The queue is arranged in order of whom she finds most desirable. The men she likes most are placed at the front, the ones she likes least are at the back.

The queue is in a constant state of flux. As she interacts with men, they may move up or down the ranks depending on how impressed she is by them. New men are constantly joining the queue, cutting in line and overtaking other men, again depending on how she feels about them.

The queue is long. Literally hundreds of men standing in line. Obviously she doesn't have time to interact with everyone in her queue, so she'll only speak to the front runners. This small group of men are the ones she'll respond to, share her number with, and accept dates from.

Her aim is to reduce this queue down to one man: the most desirable she can find. Until she finds him, she'll continue to oversee the queue's hierarchy and speak to the men near the front.

With every interaction, your place in her queue is either confirmed or moving. If she's enjoying your conversation or discovers something attractive about you, you're promoted closer to the front. If you're boring her or otherwise say/do something unattractive, you're relegated backwards.

As she interacts with other men, your position may also be adjusted. If she's just had a terrible date with the man in front of you, congratulations you've taken his spot. Or perhaps some dreamboat has sent an eye-catching opener and caught her attention, sending you backwards.

The queue is always there, even if you're never aware of it.

So how does this concept help you? It replaces the binary notion of '*she likes you/she doesn't like you*' with something a bit more nuanced and true to life. It will help explain how she interacts with you when her behaviour seems confusing or inconsistent. If you've ever wondered why a woman's interest in you blows hot and cold; sometimes interested, engaged and responsive, and at other times the opposite, your position in her queue may be the answer.

Let's take a look at a few common scenarios that may seem confusing at first, until you realise the queue is responsible for what's occurred.

### Scenario One

You've sent an opener and using the dating app's read receipt function, you see she'd viewed it almost immediately. She doesn't respond until almost a week later. Between her reading your message and replying, you'd seen she'd been online daily.

Why the delay between reading your message and responding? Most likely she didn't find you desirable enough at the time to respond immediately. You didn't quite make it into the front runner's group, but were placed high enough for a second look later. In the meantime she's interacted with the men at the front of her queue until they've disqualified themselves, either by saying or doing something she found undesirable. With them out of the way, you've been promoted towards the front of the queue.

## Messaging Strategy

> ### Scenario Two
>
> You've been chatting to a woman for a few days via the app. You haven't yet exchanged numbers, but the conversation's getting longer and more involved. Then, without warning she disappears. You can see she's online constantly, but not speaking to you. A week or so later she replies, apologising for 'ghosting' you. She says she's been really busy at work, but things are back to normal now. You continue chatting as before, exchange numbers and arrange a date.

She may have been busy with work, but chances are a man ahead of you in the queue took priority for a while. Your conversation may have ended abruptly as she wanted to dedicate more time and effort to him. Given the timescale, they may have met for a date before realising he wasn't a good match. She's finished with him and you've now taken his place in the queue.

> ### Scenario Three
>
> After a week of chatting you meet a woman for a date. It goes great. By the end you were holding hands, kissed a few times and made loose plans to meet again in the near future. The following day communication grinds to a halt. You ask how she's getting on and try making plans for next time. She can't commit to any time soon as she's busy. After a few days you don't hear from her again.

## Messaging Strategy

Until she's committed to you and quits online dating, the queue is still in operation; even after an otherwise successful date. She obviously liked you enough to get physical, but you may not have ticked all her boxes. In this case you've moved back in the queue and she'll audition the next man who's taken your spot.

Why do woman operate a queue in the first place? Isn't it easier to speak to one man at a time, and if he's not 'The One' move on to the next? Maybe, but that's a terribly inefficient strategy.

Women face a couple of issues when looking for a partner online: there are too many men, and it takes too long to gauge a man's desirability. This queuing technique allows them to screen multiple men simultaneously, prioritising those with most potential and giving enough time to see who comes out on top. It's something all women do, not out of choice but necessity.

The queue isn't unique to women either. The most desirable men, those who receive regular unsolicited messages and responses to every opener they send, also manage their own queues of women.

When interacting with any woman via online dating, ask yourself '*Where am I in her queue?*' If her responses are minimalist, or few and far between, you're clearly not at the front. However, if she's constantly messaging and fully engaged in dialogue, you may be her current front runner. This is something to especially bear in mind when you transition from your opener to a proper conversation.

# Conversational Stages And Objectives

A conversation bridges the gap between making first contact and meeting in person. With each woman you speak to online, the conversation's content will differ but its structure remains the same. All conversations pass through three potential stages, during which you will aim to complete two objectives.

### Stage One

Imagine striking up a conversation with a stranger at a bus stop. You began with:

*"Hi, I'm Dave. So which bus are you waiting for? If it's the X26 you may in for a long wait - I hear there's a diversion somewhere down the line. I'm just waiting for the 281 into town. I knew a bus driver once, he said the 281 was a nightmare to drive during rush hour..."*

The stranger on the receiving end of this monologue would most likely think 'this guy's crazy', before planning an exit strategy to get away from you.

No one in their right mind would begin a conversation with a barrage of questions, comments and observations. And yet online, plenty of men do.

The correct approach is to start with a single question or comment. When speaking to a stranger at a bus stop, that may be: *"Sorry, do you have the time?"*, or: *"Have I just missed the 281?"*, or: *"Looks like they're delayed again..."*

After initiating contact this way, the stranger will respond with their own one-liner. That's how conversations begin in 'real life', and how you should do it online - with single sentences, back and forth.

This is Stage One of the conversation; simple, short sentences. Nothing serious, no 'deep' questions, just lighthearted back and forth messaging.

Using an example from the previous chapter, if this were the hook and opener:

**Hook:** "Moved to the UK for a PhD…"
**Opener:** "Do they hand them out at Heathrow, or did you have to study for it?"

This would be the subsequent Stage One conversation:

**Her:** "No, I had to study for it :P"
**You:** "Really? Last time I went through customs they handed me a masters degree."
**Her:** "Haha I don't believe you"
**You:** "It's true - you don't get to pick which subject though, I think they hand them out at random."
**Her:** "What did you get?"
**You:** "I was given a masters in 'Interpretive Dance in Victorian Britain'."

Stage One is usually a continuation of the opener's joke/deliberate misunderstanding. This stage is short in duration, typically lasting only 3 to 5 responses from her. During this time she'll be gauging your position in her queue. How do you size up compared to the other men she's currently speaking to? Do you have potential and are you worth her time? If she decides you don't make the cut, the conversation will end here.

Most conversations will end in Stage One. Don't take it personally, just move on and continue sending openers to other women.

Don't be discouraged by her responses during this period. Like the example above, they will often be minimalistic and not give you much to work with. They may not show interest or prompt a response. So long as you're not met with obvious disinterest (consecutive one-word messages, or she tells you outright she's not into you), continue the back and forth until either she stops responding, or you enter Stage Two.

### Stage Two

Once she's established you have potential, you'll enter the second stage of the conversation. You've earned a spot near the front of her queue and now have her attention. You'll no longer have to carry the whole conversation by yourself; she's now a willing, interested participant.

You can move on from the initial opening joke and start learning about each other. This is done directly, by asking and answering questions, and indirectly, by discussing certain subjects and observing *how* each of you communicate.

As the conversation progresses, your responses will grow in length and complexity. During this stage you'll both be exchanging a paragraph or so each message; answering questions, bringing up new talking points, and asking new questions to keep the conversation flowing.

If she enjoys speaking to you, her responses will become longer and more frequent.

### Stage Three

The final stage isn't always attained and certainly not mandatory. It's only possible when you're at the very front of a woman's queue and she really enjoys communicating with you.

In the third stage each message contains multiple threads, spanning several paragraphs. By this point you'd have been speaking for a while and there's definite chemistry/attraction.

Messaging Strategy

It should be obvious you're her top contender by the length and frequency of her responses.

This period usually comes about when you're both willing to meet in person, but temporarily unable due to logistics. Rather than lose momentum, you'll continue communicating until free to attend a date. Until that time, the messages back and forth become more in depth.

**Objective One**

The first aim when chatting to women online is to move the conversation from the dating app to your mobile phone (using text/WhatsApp/Snapchat, etc). You'll want to get her number for a few reasons:

- It establishes you're interested and looking to progress things.
- If she agrees and exchanges digits it confirms she likes and trusts you. It's a positive sign she may be open to meeting in person further down the line.
- You can exchange messages in real time, not just when you're simultaneously logged into the dating app. It's much easier to keep the conversation flowing this way.
- While texting you, she's not necessarily logged into her dating profile, receiving and skim reading messages from other men. You'll have more of her attention.
- If you do arrange a date later, it's far less likely she'll stand you up if you've exchanged numbers - it displays a bit of commitment.

Some men will ask for a woman's number almost immediately after she's responded to an opener. Although this works on occasion, it's definitely not worth the gamble. Remember in Stage One she's still working out if you're worth speaking to. If you jump the gun before she's made up her mind, it's an automatic 'no'. There's no recovery from this.

Instead, Stage Two is the ideal time. By then you're building rapport and have an actual conversation going. Two or three days after her first response is the sweet spot to exchange numbers. Any sooner and she still may be hesitant, any longer she may think you're not interested.

Never ask for her number - give her yours instead. The best time to do so is at the end of a day's conversation. A simple message like: *"I'm off to bed now, but here's my number if you wanted to chat tomorrow on WhatsApp..."* works wonders. It means there's no pressure for her to give you an immediate response, and if her answer's 'no' she can hang onto your number until she feels comfortable using it. If you are turned down, it also saves you having to ask a second time.

If she does say 'no' it's for one of two reasons. Either she's cautious and wants to get to know you better, or you're not placed high enough in her queue. She may only exchange numbers with one man at a time so she isn't bombarded with texts - and you're not currently that man.

Whatever her reason for declining, never argue, complain, or ask for an explanation - even in a jokey fashion. Continue messaging as you did before. It's then your decision to pursue her further, or quit while you're ahead. You'll discover your own boundaries, but personally, if after a week of constant Stage Two conversation she's still not keen on exchanging numbers, I'd move on to someone else who shows more interest.

Another occasion to give out your number is when a conversation's drying up and you've got nothing to lose. Some women just aren't conversationalists, or don't enjoy a long, drawn out back and forth before meeting. They'd prefer to quickly exchange numbers, set up a date, and take it from there. These types of women aren't always so forward as to tell you this; you'll have to suss it out for yourself. So if in Stage Two you're not getting the kind or response you'd like, give her your number and see what happens. Usually nothing, but sometimes you'll be pleasantly surprised.

## Objective Two

The moment you've been waiting for - asking her out on a date. Before we go through the dynamics, remember going on a date is a real commitment for most women. She won't consider meeting a man by herself unless she feels she can trust him and he's worth her time. If she doesn't feel comfortable and find him desirable in some way, she won't agree to meet.

The golden rule when asking for a date is: don't bother unless you believe the answer will be an enthusiastic 'yes'. If you think she's 'on the fence' with you, due to lackadaisical or minimal responses, don't yet ask. Stage Three is the best time to invite her out. By then you're avidly messaging each other and it should be clear she likes you and enjoys speaking to you.

Unfortunately you won't reach Stage Three during every conversation, so you can't always wait for that to happen before asking. So long as you've passed Objective One and have a few days successful chatting under your belt, ask away.

When asking her on a date, be specific. Don't go with a vague: "*I was wondering if you'd like to meet up sometime?*" Instead try: "*Are you free this Saturday afternoon? Did you fancy meeting at The Embankment for a coffee?*"

The latter shows initiative and that you've taken charge. You're not loosely asking *if* she'd like to go on a date, but already have in mind a day, a time, a location, and an activity.

Women are often asked on dates by men who don't take responsibility for arranging them. These men mistakenly believe they're being chivalrous by allowing the woman to decide *all* the details. Instead, they're actually burdening them with the responsibility of arranging what they'll be doing, when and where. Never do this. If you're asking a woman on a date, you should organise it.

Being specific also allows you to gauge her interest if the answer's no. If she's keen to meet, but can't make that particular criteria, she'll agree in principle and suggest a change: *"That sounds great, but could we make it the evening instead? I'm seeing a friend that afternoon and will be busy..."*

If she's not particularly interested in meeting, she won't suggest an alternative and just give you a: *"I can't that day, I'm busy I'm afraid."* You may have to read between the lines and accept it as a polite 'No, I don't want to go on a date with you'.

Besides *how* you ask, *when* is also an important factor. If you wanted to meet on a Saturday, the optimal time to ask would be a few days beforehand, perhaps Wednesday/Thursday. If you ask too early (a week or so in advance), you may have to stretch the conversation out until then, and risk her losing interest in the meantime. If you leave it too late, she may have already made other plans.

Once you've completed Objective Two and arranged a date, continue the conversation until the big day.

CONVERSATIONAL STAGES AND OBJECTIVES

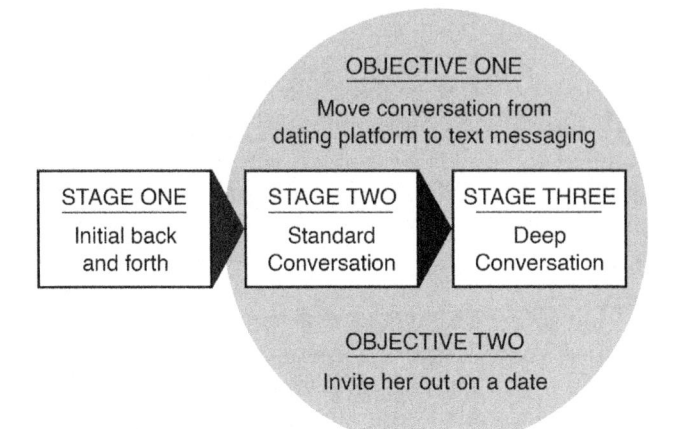

**OBJECTIVE ONE**

Move conversation from dating platform to text messaging

| STAGE ONE | STAGE TWO | STAGE THREE |
| --- | --- | --- |
| Initial back and forth | Standard Conversation | Deep Conversation |

**OBJECTIVE TWO**

Invite her out on a date

## Mastering Conversations

It takes practice to effectively communicate via the written word. Luckily, with your attractive profile and impactful openers, you'll have plenty of opportunity to learn the craft. You'll soon discover for yourself what works, and more importantly what doesn't. Until then here's some practical advice, giving you a head start on mastering text conversations.

### Keep it Lighthearted

You want the conversation's mood to be enjoyable and entertaining. If the topics discussed are too somber or overly serious, she'll become disengaged. Online dating ought to be a way to escape life's daily drudgery, meet someone special and fall in love. Discussing what's wrong with the world takes the shine off that exciting prospect. Keep it playful, keep it fun.

### Questions & Answers

You may be keen to learn about each other before deciding to meet in person, but don't reduce the conversation to bland exchange of personal details. Asking and answering questions is an important part of the conversation stage, but ensure the chat doesn't become a monotonous Q&A session.

It's not a job interview, where the aim is to reel off a series of probing questions to assess someone's suitability. Besides the usual factoids, you should also share opinions, thoughts and even stories to create an enjoyable connection.

## Joint Enterprise

Use the conversation to build a narrative where you're partnered up in some capacity. I use this technique in one of the example openers:

**Hook:** "Looking for a committed relationship, not just a 'partner in crime'."
**Opener:** "That's a shame. My heist needs a getaway driver and we thought you'd fit the bill."

There's so much scope here to build a story together: what are you actually stealing, what's her payment, what happened to the previous getaway driver, will you be wearing disguises, what happens if you're caught...

The best conversations are those littered with these imaginary dramas. These stories can be apropos of nothing, like the above example, or based on information in her profile/a subject that arises in conversation. By inventing these scenarios together you're establishing private jokes and building a relationship of sorts before you've even met.

## Music

If there's one topic everyone has an opinion on and enjoys discussing, it's their favourite music. This is an excellent Stage Two subject to explore. Ask what she's currently listening to and share a couple of tracks from your own playlist. Exchanging music is a great way to build rapport, get to know each other better and discover new bands/songs you'd never heard before.

## Heir and a Spare

Always aim to have two Stage Two/Three conversations running simultaneously. You may feel uncomfortable speaking to two women at once, but there are good reasons to do so.

- Don't be under any illusion you're the only man she's speaking to. Remember the queue; just because you're at the front, it doesn't mean you'll stay there. Even when conversations (or dates for that matter) go well, something better may catch her eye and you'll be quickly replaced. Don't expect, or give, any sort of loyalty until you've established a monogamous relationship.

- If a connection with a woman has run its course, either because the conversation has dried up or a date didn't go well, you won't have to start the process all over again. You'll have someone else to speak to and won't feel that sense of loss/rejection so keenly. It's easier to maintain momentum with dating apps if you're never having to go back to scratch.

- When speaking to one woman only, it can be difficult to not come across too keen. When all your energy is dedicated to one conversation, you'll be replying quickly and with more enthusiasm than usual. It's easy to become over-invested and chase her away with undesirable eagerness. Speaking with two women simultaneously keeps you busy and instils in you an abundance mentality. By not investing too much in any one conversation, you'll come across as more relaxed and attractive for it.

- Limit yourself to two conversations at any one time. Any more and you'll become overwhelmed. You'll start to forget which woman said what and get mixed up. It's only a matter of time before you embarrass yourself by repeating subjects, asking the same questions twice, or mistaking one woman for another.

**Match Her Investment**

During Stage Two pay attention to the length of her messages and how quickly she responds. You'll want to keep yours at a similar size and pace. For example, if she takes a couple of hours to respond with two sentences, don't reply immediately with several paragraphs. Instead, message at a more leisurely pace with a few sentences of your own. You don't have to get the stopwatch out or perform a word count, but keep it in the same ballpark. If not, you may come across too keen.

### Compliments

As one of the terrible opening gambits, you'll know to avoid compliments when making first contact, but what about during the conversation? The only time it's safe to do so is during Stage Three, where you've built rapport and there's obvious attraction/chemistry. Any time prior to this and you're still subject to the trifecta of reasons compliments don't work: she hears them all the time, your sincerity is questionable, and she may not be attracted to you.

There's also a risk your well intentioned words miss the mark. You could remark how amazing she looks in that profile picture with the red dress, but she may interpret that as you being a creep and ogling her photos. It's best to keep compliments to yourself, unless she compliments you first.

### Sexual Language

From playful innuendo, to full on 'sexting', let her dictate what's acceptable when it comes to adult conversation. Never initiate it. Most women won't feel comfortable discussing sex over text messages with a man she's never met. Some have no issues with it and at Stage Three may ask what kind of things you're into, or their flirting may become increasingly risqué, but they're a minority. For many women, sexual messages during the conversation stage is a dealbreaker. If you go down that route she may become uncomfortable and end your connection.

### Complaining

Never question her lack of response or complain she isn't communicating as much or as often as you'd like. Even if framed in a jokey way, it comes across as desperate and needy. Lamenting she's not as engaged in the conversation as you are isn't going to improve things - she'll simply withdraw further.

Either accept she's not a great communicator/you're not a priority for her, or end the conversation yourself.

## Ideal Topics

*"Great minds discuss ideas, average minds discuss events, small minds discuss people"* - a quote often attributed to Eleanor Roosevelt. Sound advice if you're ever invited to the White House, but for online dating the opposite applies. Save the ideas (politics, philosophy, religion, etc) and events (current affairs outside your own personal life) for when you meet in person. When texting, it's more enjoyable and engaging to discuss the day-to-day goings on with your life and the people in it, rather than your views on neoclassical economic theory.

## Humour

You want the conversation to be playful and fun, but take care when employing humour. Without the visual cues of a face-to-face interaction, it can be hard sometimes to discern if someone is joking or being sarcastic. Jokes can also be lost in translation if the woman you're messaging isn't a native English speaker. Humour is also subjective; what you find hilarious she may find cringy, or mean, or pedestrian.

## Double Texting

If at any stage of your conversation she fails to respond, the conversation's over. Sending a second message hoping to prompt a reply is a waste of time. No matter how busy she is, if you're high enough in her queue, she'll never 'leave you on read' and forget to message back. If it's been a few days and she still hasn't got back to you, cut your losses and move on. She isn't so busy, she hasn't forgotten, nothing's happened to her... you're just no longer a priority.

By not 'double texting', you're also leaving the door open for her to rekindle the conversation in the following weeks if her queue's front runners have fallen by the wayside.

## Proofread

As your messages increase in length, so do the chances of spelling mistakes, grammatical errors, or falling foul of autocorrect. To keep on top of this, write those longer messages on your phone's notepad app first. This way it's much easier to edit your response, you don't have to write and send the message in one sitting, and it also removes the possibility of accidentally sending an unfinished text.

## Ending Conversations

If during Stage Two things aren't going anywhere, don't flog a dead horse. If you're not near the front of the queue, she may be doing the bare minimum to keep you in line. Instead of maintaining a one-sided conversation, simply stop responding. You'll be met with one of two outcomes. Either you'll never hear from her again, in which case it was only a matter of time before that happened anyway, or after a week or two she'll reconnect, usually with more interest this time. Ironically, ceasing communication with a woman can sometimes improve your position in her queue. It implies you're busy elsewhere and have other options - an attractive trait.

It won't be long before you 'click' with a woman and the conversation flows effortlessly. Once you've agreed to meet it's time to prepare for the next stage - The Date.

## Chapter Summary

- Avoid the 'Five Terrible Opening Gambits': solitary 'hellos', generic copy/pasted messages, paragraphs of introductory text, compliments/sexual messages, and anything angry/abusive.

- Only send Impactful Openers when making first contact: short, snappy messages bespoke to the recipient that grab attention and are easy for her to reply to.

- Make a game out of sending Impactful Openers. Don't concentrate on the response rate, instead think about how many messages you can send in a limited time for example.

- Once you've successfully made contact, a conversation is necessary for you to demonstrate your desirability and build attraction.

- A conversation's made up of three stages: an initial back and forth of short messages leading on from the opener, then a real conversation where you can get to know each other better, finally culminating (though not always) in a deep chat where each message contains multiple talking points and it's obvious there's attraction and real interest between you.

- At any point, the conversation may come to an abrupt end. In this case, accept it and simply move on to other women.

- There are two objectives during a conversation: move the dialogue from the online dating platform to text messaging, and later asking her out on a date.

- 'The Queue' is a concept that allows you to understand and gauge a woman's behaviour from when you first make contact, right up to establishing a relationship. You are always competing for a woman's attention from other men. She is looking for the best man possible; your job is to ensure that's you.

PART 5

# Meeting In Person

# Meeting In Person

```
                    /\
                   /  \
                  /    \
                 /  5.  \
                / MEETING\
               / IN PERSON\
              /------------\
             / 4. MESSAGING \
            /    STRATEGY    \
           /------------------\
          /   3. ONLINE DATING \
         /----------------------\
        /     2. BECOMING A       \
       /      DESIRABLE MAN        \
      /------------------------------\
     /    1. WHAT DO WOMEN WANT       \
    /----------------------------------\
```
(6. DATING MASTERY surrounds the pyramid)

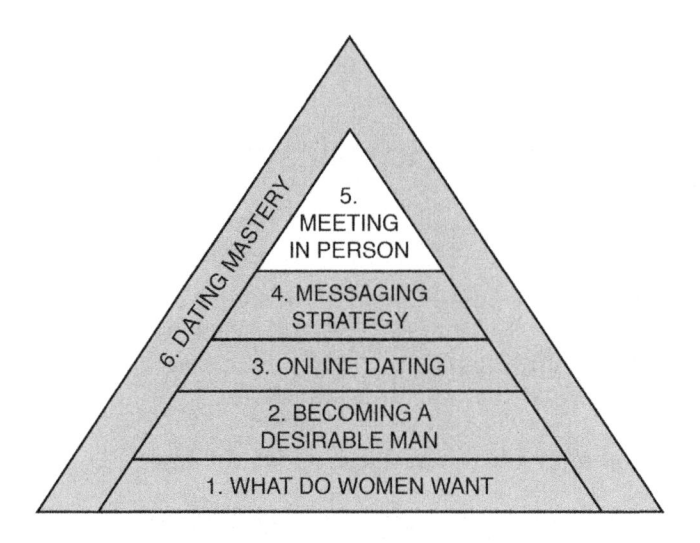

A first date could be the most important event of your life. You may be meeting your future wife/life partner/mother of your children for the very first time. But for that *happily ever after* to happen, you'll have to make a positive first impression.

If you've followed my guidance so far, you should be in a great position to do so. You'll know what women find attractive and have worked on becoming a desirable man. Prior to meeting you've hopefully built rapport and established some chemistry via text messaging. Now it's up to you to seal the deal and make this first date a success.

This chapter will guide you through the logistics of dating, ensuring you both have a great time and generate that spark necessary to begin a relationship.

# Basic Dating Logistics

When inviting a woman on a date, it's your role to take charge and organise it. But before you start racking your brain for brilliant activities or places to visit, let's take a step back and think about what makes a date successful.

By the end of an ideal first date you would have:

- Both expressed you like each other and have enjoyed each other's company.
- Established a romantic connection, not just a potential friendship. This means flirting, touching, hand-holding, hugging and/or kissing.
- Made solid plans to meet again soon to progress the relationship.

With these outcomes in mind, you have a blueprint for your first date. You must arrange a meeting that gives you the best chance of achieving these results. The following factors will play huge part in facilitating this.

**Duration**

No matter how great your text conversation, it will take time to transition from almost stranger to love interest. So if your date has a restrictive time limit, it will prove difficult to build a connection and meet those goals.

A good first date will last a couple of hours, a great one can last several. So don't plan to meet too late in the day, or knowing one of you has a prior engagement and can only spare thirty minutes for a quick coffee.

Ideally pick a day you're both free from work/obligations and meet in the early afternoon. This way there's scope to extend the date into the evening and beyond if things go well. If this isn't possible, at the very least allow for a couple of hours potential time together.

## Verbal Communication

In order to build any kind of connection, you must be able to speak to each other freely. Unsuccessful dates usually involve stifled conversation. Sometimes this is due to a lack of experience or attraction for the other person, but it can be caused by logistics. Below are common obstacles to productive and enjoyable conversations.

- The environment is too loud, making it a struggle to hear each other
- There's something else you're both intently focused on, preventing you from chatting
- There's a lack of privacy, where others can clearly eavesdrop on your conversation

If a venue or activity ticks any of these boxes, it's not suitable for a first date.

## Non-Verbal Communication

Researchers estimate non-verbal accounts for anywhere between 50% to 90% of all in-person communication. This means body language, eye contact, facial expressions and hand gestures are all vital to making a good first impression. You must be able to read and telegraph these non-verbal cues during a date. The same goes for touch; from an initial greeting hug, to flirty arm/leg touches, to potentially holding hands and more. If you're not in a position to do these things, then your date may as well be a phone call.

### Enjoyable Environment

Any first date activity, event or location must be an enjoyable one. Things won't end well unless you're both comfortable, relaxed and happy in whatever you're doing together. With this in mind, avoid the following:

- Plans that involve a hobby or pastime she doesn't already partake in. Likewise for anything that requires lots of skill or previous experience to enjoy.
- A scenario where you're both 'stuck' at a venue/activity for an extended period without an easy way to leave.
- A physical activity she wasn't prepared for, or anything that requires particular clothing/footwear.

These basic logistics are pivotal in determining a successful date. You could be a perfect match with someone, but if your first date is: too short in duration, you can't easily see/hear/touch each other, the environment/activity is uncomfortable, then you're never going to 'click' and get a second date.

It's important to plan ahead and account for those factors. If not, you're needlessly setting yourself up for a disappointing outcome.

## Creating A Scene

Imagine your first date as a movie. There are two main characters and they'll be spending a couple of hours on screen together. If this film comprised a single scene, where they remained in situ and held an uninterrupted, two hour dialogue... it would be a box office flop. It doesn't matter how great the script is or how much chemistry the actors have, after a short while it would become quite tedious.

Meeting In Person

First dates are much like movies: they require multiple scenes to help progress the story and hold our interest. The scenes don't have to be action-packed, or even all that memorable. There just has to be a sequence of them linked together for us to remain engaged.

Consider the examples below. In both scenarios Adam and Sue are meeting for the first time. After connecting online, they've arranged a coffee date at a local town.

> ### Date A
>
> Adam and Sue agree to meet at 3pm at the Steamy Beans Café in Kingston. Adam arrives early and finds an empty table by the window. He orders himself a coffee and waits for Sue.
> She arrives fifteen minutes later. Adam greets Sue as she enters the café. They visit the counter together where Adam buys a round of drinks.
>
> They sit facing each other at the table, sip their coffees and chat for 45 minutes. It's an enjoyable conversation, but Sue doesn't feel a romantic spark.
> Sue makes her excuses and tells Adam she has to leave - she has plans for later.
>
> Adam and Sue leave the café together. They share a quick hug before going their separate ways.

Adam didn't do anything wrong here per se. He was able to keep the conversation going and managed to avoid any awkward silences. However, the date felt a little formal - like a job interview. He knew there wasn't a romantic connection, so wasn't surprised when Sue asked if they could 'just be friends' when he later enquired about meeting again.

Meeting In Person

Let's compare this to a different scenario.

> ### Date B
> 
> Adam and Sue agree to meet for a coffee at 3pm in Kingston. At Adam's suggestion they meet by the train station, as there are several great cafés in the area and they could choose one on the day.
> 
> They meet, share a quick hug and make their way towards the high street. En route Adam stops at an ATM to make a cash withdrawal.
> 
> Walking up the high street together, they agree on visiting the Steamy Beans Café. After a five minute stroll, they reach the venue. They find a table inside and Adam buys a round of drinks.
> They sit facing each other, sip their coffees and chat for 45 minutes. During their conversation, Adam shares his favourite author was about to release a new title. He wanted to visit a bookshop on the high street to see when it's available.
> 
> Sue explains she can't stay out long due to plans later, but would like to accompany him in the bookshop before ending their date.
> 
> They leave the café together and walk down the high street. They enter a local bookshop and browse for a while before Adam makes his enquiry with a member of staff.
> 
> After discovering the book is released next week, they leave the shop. Adam walks Sue back to the station. Once there, they share a quick hug before going their separate ways.

Irrespective of the outcome, this date was a huge improvement over the first example. Both were simple coffee dates, lasting an hour or so, but 'Date A' comprised a single scene. The whole event began and ended in the same place - the coffee shop. This gave Adam almost no opportunity to transform the date from a friendly conversation into something more romantic.

In comparison, 'Date B' took Adam and Sue through multiple scenes. From their first meeting at the train station, to the ATM, the café, the book shop, and finally back to the train station. Additionally, there were scenes between those venues - the walk from each place to the next.

Organising a first date with multiple scenes is essential for a few reasons:

- You can naturally extend the date, one scene at a time. When inviting a woman to meet, you would never ask them to spend five hours with you right off the bat. You would, for example, just arrange to meet for a coffee. And if that coffee goes well, it becomes a walk around town, then a visit to a local museum, and then getting dinner, and then a couple of drinks... and before you know it, you've spent five hours together. Something she wouldn't have agreed to before meeting
Conversely, if a date goes poorly, you can end it with minimal fuss. If you planned to spend a whole afternoon at a local fair with a woman, it's difficult to leave 20 minutes into the date after discovering she's not your cup of tea. However, if the plan was to meet for an ice cream, there's no issue making your excuses and saying goodbye once you've finished your cone.

- When a location isn't logistically ideal, it's not such a problem. In the above scenarios, if the Steamy Beans Café was too loud to chat comfortably, it would have completely ruined 'Date A'. Not so for 'Date B', which had multiple scenes before and after the café visit. If a particular activity/event/location doesn't allow you to communicate effectively, or prevents you from engaging with your date, it's not the end of the world. Simply change scenes when the opportunity arises and progress the date from there.

It's difficult to find a single activity/event/location that ticks all the ideal logistical boxes, but when your date comprises multiple scenes, you don't have to. So long as during the course of the date you're able to: speak to each other, have some privacy, display/read each others' body language, etc, then it's fine.

- It's far less likely the conversation will run dry. A change of scenery always prompts something new to discuss. Even something as mundane as visiting an ATM to withdraw cash presents plenty of conversational opportunity. Adam could joke with Sue, asking her to keep lookout so he doesn't get robbed. Or discuss the irrational fear everyone has at some point of forgetting their PIN or having their card 'swallowed' by the machine.

If you're struggling with awkward silences during a date, don't think about new topics to discuss or questions to ask - think about changing the scene. The conversation will then take care of itself.

Creating a date with multiple scenes is the best way to ensure a successful outing. A few changes of scenery will help keep you both entertained and engaged throughout your time together. In the following pages, I'll also show how it can assist in establishing a romantic connection.

## Building Attraction

Most men have two aims during a date: demonstrate what a great guy they are, and ensure the woman has an enjoyable time. They believe if these bases are sufficiently covered, their date will feel chemistry and she'll be open to pursuing something romantic.

Unfortunately this is seldom the case. The above aims are an excellent way to make new friends, but not so great for getting *girlfriends*. If you want a date to see you as a potential love interest and not just as a friend, then you must also *build attraction*.

This isn't something that occurs by osmosis. Simply spending time together doesn't guarantee she'll develop romantic feelings for you. You must interact with her in a way that shows you're partner material and that you're interested in her.

## Attraction Timeline

At some point during your date you'll have to 'make your move' and indicate you want to be more than just friends. If not, you may miss the opportunity and she'll promote the next man in her queue who won't be so diffident.

Knowing when and how to escalate things is perhaps the most daunting part of a date. Do you put your arm around her, hold her hand, go in for a kiss? If so, when exactly? It's crucial you get this right; every interaction since your first opening message has been leading up to this moment. Before we learn the correct method to making your move, let's see how men often get it wrong.

### *Delegate*

> A common mistake is to leave the woman in charge of expressing romantic interest. Men will rationalise their lack of action in a couple of ways: by thinking it's somehow courteous to let the woman make the first move, or by telling themselves if she doesn't escalate things she clearly isn't interested.

### *Delay*

> Some men will procrastinate until the very last moment before escalating. They'll display no romantic interest throughout an entire date, before suddenly

going full steam ahead and attempting a kiss as they're saying goodbye.

## *Defer*

Others will think of the first date as a 'warm up', to establish a friendship of sorts before really attempting to woo her on the second (or third, or fourth...) meeting. Until then, they'll show no romantic interest, worried they'll come across as improper and potentially scare their date away.

## *Disproportionate*

The above mistakes are borne from the same cause: a fear of rejection. Those who fear it most will defer and delegate. Those slightly braver will delay, hoping to minimise the consequences of a potential rejection. The final common mistake, a disproportionate one, doesn't come from fear, but a lack of judgment. They come on too strong, too quickly - attempting to get physical long before it's appropriate and their date feels comfortable doing so.

Given these pitfalls, how and when should one 'make their move' and show interest? The correct answer isn't to make a move at all, but to build attraction gradually throughout the date. There should be no single defining event that elevates things from friendly to romantic, but a series of incremental steps. The first of which is flirting.

## Flirting

Flirting is any behaviour used to show sexual interest in another person. It's a way of advertising '*I like you*' without having to spell it out overtly. Flirting allows us to test the waters and see if someone's feelings are reciprocated. If so, they'll respond with their own flirty behaviour.
Some common methods of flirting are:

- Compliments - especially on someone's appearance or attributes that are considered attractive (e.g. physical strength in a man).
- Frequent smiling and laughing during conversation.
- Eye contact - either staring at the person more than usual, or the opposite: repeatedly looking away and back again due to shyness.
- Change in vocal tone - men's voices tend to go deeper and women's higher than their usual pitch when speaking to someone they are interested in.
- Gift giving or performing small tasks/favours for a person.
- Sexual conversation - discussing their likes/dislikes/previous experiences, or jokes of a sexual nature e.g. double entendres.
- Joint Enterprise - as described in the Messaging Strategy chapter, building a narrative via conversation where you're partnered up in some capacity.

Recognising these behaviours and being able to perform them is the first step to building attraction. But like any social interaction it will take practice and experience to get right.

Men typically struggle with flirting for a few reasons:

- It's easy to misinterpret a woman's behaviour. You may think she's flirting when she isn't, or not realise she's flirting when she is. There's no one-size-fits-all answer to this potential misunderstanding. Is she attracted to you, or just being friendly? It depends entirely on the context. If you're on a date, the above behaviours are a great indicator she likes you and is flirting. However, if it's a female friend/colleague who smiles, laughs at your jokes and gives you a hug when saying hello - she may do this with everyone and is simply being friendly.
- Studies have shown men and woman flirt for different reasons. For men it's quite straightforward: we'll only flirt with women whom we find attractive. But for

women, that isn't the case. They'll also flirt to strengthen friendships with men, to practice their own flirting technique, and also for fun. So a woman may genuinely flirt with you, but it doesn't necessarily mean she finds you attractive.

- Due to a lack of experience or knowhow, some men employ feminine flirting behaviours in an attempt to build attraction. This includes: acting shy/embarrassed/overawed when communicating; unnecessary compliments; or becoming agreeable and conceding that her opinions/preferences/wants etc are superior to his own ("*You have much better taste in music than me...*"). These are submissive flirting behaviours. Men find these attractive in potential partners but women don't.

The first step to flirting during a date is to create an environment where you can both enjoy each other's company, smile, and laugh. It's almost impossible to flirt if the atmosphere is serious and businesslike. The conversation should be fun and lighthearted.

Once you've set the tone, this leads nicely to the next step in building attraction - teasing.

**Teasing**

When the opportunity arises, you shouldn't be afraid to tease your date. By this I mean having fun with her, sometimes at her expense, in a playful and lighthearted fashion. This demonstrates confidence and shows you aren't some submissive panderer desperate to gain her favour.

Teasing is a misunderstood concept for many, especially those who are *au fait* with modern dating advice. 'Negging', a term popularised by 'Pick Up Artists', is a bastardisation of teasing. But the two are often mistakenly synonymous.

Teasing is lighthearted, and should never be used to cause offence or undermine a woman. It ought to be playful and fun:

like friends gently ribbing each other over some minor mishap or comical mistake.

Negging on the other hand is a deliberate attempt to undermine a woman's confidence, often with underhanded compliments.

To give examples of both:

> ### Teasing
>
> As Sue attempts to drink her coffee, she accidentally spills some on her lap. Adam passes a handful of tissues and reassures her with faux sympathy: *"It's ok, it can't be easy handling cups with those tiny hands. It'll take practice."*

Adam has diffused a potentially embarrassing situation for Sue with a tease. He'd implied spilling coffee wasn't a clumsy act, but obviously due to Sue having tiny hands. The idea Sue's hands are too small to operate a cup is comical, as is Adam's encouragement she'll get better with practice.

The joke was at Sue's expense, but wasn't mean. Had Adam suggested Sue's hands were large (and therefore manly), then it would have been a different story.

> ### Negging
>
> As conversation turned to pre-date routines and 'glamming up' to meet new people, Sue has explained her eye makeup technique. Adam responds with sarcasm: *"You're brave trying a style like that - especially on a first date."*

Adam's implied Sue's makeup is unattractive and a mistake had she hoped to make a good first impression. It's a tongue in cheek comment but has a lot of potential to cause offence. If Sue were supremely confident and *knew* she looked amazing, she'd interpret Adam's words as an ironic joke. However, if she were a little unsure of herself (as most of us are) chances are she'd take Adam's words literally - as unwarranted criticism.

With negging, the recipient's perception of the joke is irrelevant; it doesn't matter if the woman finds the joke funny or hurtful. It's the skewed idea that knocking a woman's confidence with 'humorous' observations will somehow make her keen to earn your approval.

Imagine a date joking that you were lazy, or had a low status job. No matter how funny or witty the comment, it wouldn't endear you to her - quite the opposite.

Teasing is nothing like this. It's a way of playing with your date, having fun and sharing a wry sense of humour. It's not a psychopathic attempt to manipulate women into liking you.

You can gauge how well your teasing is received by her reaction. If she laughs, sarcastically reprimands you, playful hits/pretends to hit you, or best of all counters with her own teasing, then she likes you. When this is the case you should move on to the next step in the attraction ladder.

As important as teasing is in establishing a romantic connection, it isn't mandatory. For some men it's just not in their nature. And some women, especially those of a serious disposition, won't be receptive to, or reciprocate in teasing - no matter how attracted they are to you. So try it once if the opportunity arises but if you're met with a stoney face, accept she isn't the teasing type.

## Proximity and Touching

Within half hour of meeting you should be able to gauge how well things are going. If the conversation is flowing nicely, with intermittent laughing, joking and preferably teasing, it's time to think about becoming physical.

If, however, this isn't the case, then do not attempt to take things further. When your date is serious/uninterested/unresponsive, then accept this isn't going anywhere. Continue to keep things friendly until the date naturally peters out and it's time to part ways.

Moving up a gear from verbal to physical flirting is an incremental process. It begins by decreasing the distance between yourselves, then to casual touching, and finally culminates with hand holding. The below example demonstrates this transition from flirting to holding hands.

> ### *Date C*
>
> Adam and Sue meet at the Steamy Beans café for their first date. After ordering drinks, they find a small two-seater table. They sit opposite each other and engage in conversation.
>
> Their meeting goes well. They've been able to build on the connection they'd made via text messaging and are enjoying each other's company.
>
> The pair have shown interest in each other through intermittent flirting.
>
> - Sue had complimented Adam on his shirt.
> - Adam responded by applauding Sue on her taste in men's shirts (a tease - he's subverted expectation to praise something she's wearing in return).

- They've continued inside jokes established when text messaging.
- Adam had teased Sue for getting lost en route to the date and being 10 minutes late.
- Sue's riposte was she wasn't lost at all, but running late from a prior date with another (more handsome) man.

After finishing their coffees, the pair agreed to explore a local park. Whilst strolling together, Adam closes the gap between them so they are walking almost shoulder to shoulder. They continue joking with each other. At one point Sue almost trips over a kerb. Adam places his hand on her shoulder and offers to find Sue a walking stick. Sue retaliates at the tease by gently shoving Adam.

After a lap around the park, they visit a local pub. They find a sofa and sit next to each other.
During conversation, Adam momentarily places his hand on Sue's knee to emphasise a point in the story he's telling.

After finishing their drinks, they leave the pub and walk towards their next venue. Whilst walking side by side, Adam holds Sue's hand. Sue gently squeezes Adam's hand confirming she's happy with this development.

Two key points from this story:

> **1)** By slowly escalating the flirting, Adam was able to gauge when Sue was comfortable with his advances and could progress accordingly. Had he attempted to hold Sue's hand immediately after leaving the Steamy Beans café, she probably wouldn't have responded so positively and pulled her hand away.

Once Adam had established Sue was receptive to verbal flirting, he knew he could escalate by moving physically closer to her. He did this by walking almost shoulder to shoulder with her through the park. Had Sue felt uncomfortable with this proximity, she would have moved away from Adam and maintained a couple of feet distance from him. Adam was able to reaffirm this comfort by sharing a sofa in the pub.

Satisfied Sue was happy to be near him, Adam introduced casual touching to the conversation. He momentarily placed his hand on Sue's shoulder in the park, and again on her knee in the pub. He didn't attempt to make the touch sexual in any way by holding his hand there for too long or by stroking/squeezing. Adam also didn't go overboard by touching Sue too often. Twice was enough for him to gauge her reaction and to let Sue know he likes her.

On both occasions Sue's response was positive: she didn't move away or show any signs of awkwardness or discomfort. She reciprocated with a casual touch of her own by playfully shoving Adam in the park.

Having passed those checkpoints: from verbal flirting, to close proximity, to casual touching, Adam could then hold Sue's hand confident she would be receptive to it.

**2)** The catalyst to this escalation was a regular change of scene, with particular importance on walking together from one place to the next. Had Adam and Sue's date been entirely at the Steamy Beans café, no matter how well they got on verbally, it would have been incredibly difficult to escalate physically. Adam could have moved his chair closer to Sue's but rearranging furniture is awkward. It could also come across as too keen - and prevented Sue from giving negative feedback, as she's unlikely to pick up her chair and move it away from Adam's.

> Whilst walking together Adam was able to gauge how comfortable Sue was with his proximity. He also had easier access to casual touching, and when the time was right, could hold hands with minimal fuss or awkwardness.

Becoming physical with your date needn't be a haphazard gamble. It should be a methodical, natural process of moving closer to them, casual touching, and finally holding hands. At each stage monitor her response. If she maintains her distance, responds awkwardly to any casual touch, or stops flirting verbally, then stop escalating and move back a stage.

Multiple scenes in a date are essential to building attraction. Without them, escalating physically can be almost impossible. If you're never in a position to move closer to your date how can you expect to hold hands with her? Ideally changing scenes is done by moving to a new venue, but sometimes that's not possible. If there's nowhere else to go from your current location because you're in a quiet part of town say, or it's late and everything's closed, then you'll have to improvise.

If you're at a bar for example, this could mean changing your seating location. When sat at a table, move to the bar area, or a private booth. Or if there are activities, like a pool table or darts board, give those a try. Anything that gets you out of your seats and moving is infinitely better than sitting in one spot for an entire date.

### *Personal Experience*

I used to be completely ignorant of the need to build attraction during dates. I was of the mindset that once you'd met in person, a woman either likes you or she doesn't. I believed that 'spark' or 'chemistry' or whatever you want to call it, was entirely out of my control. I could only show up to a date, be myself, and hope for the best.

I was confident to flirt verbally, make women laugh and even tease where appropriate, but more often than not, that wasn't enough. By the end of a typical date, I'd return home none the wiser as to how she felt about me. I didn't realise it then, but most of these women would have felt much the same way about me and my feelings towards them. Because I hadn't escalated much beyond being friendly, my dates would be forgiven for thinking I wasn't interested in them romantically.

I needed a way to bridge the gap between being friendly and being 'interested'. Casual touching was that intermediate step. Unlike attempting to hold hands, or going for a kiss, casual touching is completely non-committal. If a date didn't respond positively to a casual touch, it wouldn't become an elephant in the room and ruin our time together.

Whenever a date was going well, I would set myself a target of three casual touches. If I could perform those without receiving negative feedback (a change in her body language showing disinterest, like leaning away/creating distance between us, or no longer engaging in flirting/teasing conversational cues) then I would be confident to escalate and hold her hand.

This was a game changer for me as my success rate on dates increased exponentially. I'd discovered casual touching was an essential component for building attraction. Without it, I was dependant on my date to 'make the first move' and show interest.
Additionally, I never had an unsatisfactory ending to a date after I'd employed casual touching. I'd always know for sure if she was interested in me or not. I didn't have to second guess her feelings because I'd escalated enough during the date to get an answer.

The art to casual touching is knowing when to do so. It has to be as natural as possible, and as mentioned above, mustn't be perceived as sexual in any way. A few personal examples:

- If a date compliments my jacket, I'll return the kind words: "*It's not as nice as yours... where did you get it from?*" and I'll feel her sleeve.

- If we're at a venue and I need to use the toilet, I'll excuse myself with a joke: "*If you run off while I'm gone, please don't steal my umbrella.*" Whilst touching her upper arm for a second.

- If we're at a bar and she's undecided between a soft drink or something stronger, I touch her shoulder momentarily and say: "*If you're feeling gin, go for it.*"

None of these examples are romantic magical moments, but that's the point. They're just a way to demonstrate interest, and see how comfortable she is with your non-affectionate touching before escalating.

If she's attracted to you, the casual touching is often reciprocated. She'll think of ways to touch you, or excuses for you to touch her. For example, one creative date used the palm of my hand to trace out a map with her finger. Occasionally I'm asked to help adjust a date's clothing, like tucking in collar labels, or checking hard-to-reach zips are secured.

So if your dates are going well but you're struggling to escalate things, ensure casual touching is in your repertoire of attraction tactics. It will make a world of difference to your dating outcomes.

## Kissing

The final stop on the attraction timeline is kissing. If you've successfully navigated the above route from flirting, to casual touching, to hand-holding, then going in for that first kiss won't be such a daunting step.

As a rule of thumb, if a date is happy to hold hands, she'll be comfortable with a kiss. By this stage, the date has clearly gone well and she's attracted to you. But before attempting to lock lips, there are a few pointers to bear in mind.

- Think about your location, specifically, who else is around you. Being conscious of potential voyeurs nearby can ruin the mood and make your date reluctant to kiss. Ideally you want a location where you're entirely by yourselves and can enjoy privacy. Alternatively, a venue that's so busy no one will be paying any attention to you - like a transport hub during peak time for instance.

- Don't wait for the very last moment of a date to kiss. The location may not be ideal and you'll both wish you had done so earlier. Once you've established she's comfortable holding hands, then wait half an hour or so and then think about when and where to kiss.

- Don't ask your date for permission to kiss her. You may think it's gentlemanly, but in reality it signals indecisiveness and a lack of confidence - both unattractive traits. If she flirts with you, engages in casual touching and is holding your hand, you don't need any more green lights. If by this stage she still doesn't want to kiss you, she will turn her cheek and allow you to kiss that - it's not an issue.

### *The Attraction Timeline In Action*

In an ideal world, you'll part ways after a first date having escalated from flirting to sharing a kiss or two. But in reality, that won't always happen. Any hurdles to completing the attraction timeline will fall into one of two categories:

### *She's just not into you*

It may be upsetting, especially after a promising back and forth whilst texting, but you're not going to be everyone's cup of tea. If your date shows no signs of flirting, doesn't respond well to an attempted tease, and is generally distant and businesslike in conversation, then accept it isn't going anywhere.

It isn't always so obvious when a woman isn't attracted to you. Many men mistake friendliness for sexual interest, especially when a woman has agreed to a date, and so shown an initial fancy. Women are averse to confrontation, and won't often give a clear, unprompted rejection unless pushed to it. A lack of any progress on the attraction timeline, no matter how friendly she is otherwise, is the best barometer for gauging her interest in you.

### *She likes you, but...*

Some dates may not end with a kiss, but there was still progress made on the attraction timeline. Perhaps you got as far as mutual flirting, close proximity or casual touching before home time. In these cases, there could be several reasons for the limited progress. On the more pessimistic side, there could be another man in the queue whom your date wants to meet before escalating with you. Maybe she doesn't feel comfortable holding hands and kissing if she's still weighing up her options between a couple of suitors.

But equally possible are the optimistic grounds: she prefers to take things slower, the logistics weren't right, or you weren't bold enough to escalate.

Every woman you'll meet is unique. Some are keen to hold hands and kiss within an hour of meeting. Others would never dream of kissing on a first date - no matter how attracted she was to you.

On the logistics side, if your date is too brief there won't be enough time to escalate. You can't expect to get physical over a single coffee. It will take time and a few changes of scene to reach the final step and kiss. Additionally the location may not be suitable to escalate. For most of us, displaying physical affection is a private matter; we won't do so in front of an unwitting audience.

And finally, you may walk away without kissing due to your own lack of action. You may not have been bold enough to hold hands, or maybe you got that far and didn't know when to attempt a kiss. In those situations, don't berate yourself - there's always next time. It takes practice and experience before you're confident to capitalise on every opportunity.

There's no strict timescale to follow when building attraction. If your date really likes you and you're competently escalating, you may be holding hands and kissing within a hour of meeting. Though as a rough guide it will most likely take two to four hours to complete the timeline. There should be no rush in doing so. Allow your date to set the pace with her feedback. If she's flirty right from the start, then don't hesitate to close the proximity when able. If she takes a while to relax and become comfortable in your presence, then take it slowly.

If you haven't completed the attraction timeline during the first date, continue where you left off on the second meeting. You should always aim to have concluded the attraction timeline before the end of a second date, unless there are extenuating circumstances. For example, if she's had a particularly strict or religious upbringing, she may never feel comfortable kissing in public. When something like this is the case, she'll more than likely let you know - especially if she likes you and doesn't want you to think otherwise.

If you don't secure a kiss before the end of a second date and you're the stumbling block, you run the risk of her losing patience. She won't remain interested forever.

### *Personal Experience*

Each date you attend will be a learning experience. Even if it's a lesson on how *not* to do something. A couple of anecdotes spring to mind when I think about building attraction and the attraction timeline.

On one particular first date things were going terribly. We'd exchanged messages for a week or so prior to meeting and seemed to get on well via text. However, in person the dialogue was painfully slow. Despite my best efforts, it was more like a job interview than a date. I'd tried every conversational trick in my bag: flirted and teased when the opportunity arose, changed scenes a couple of times, but nothing. It was obvious she wasn't interested.

After a couple of hours together, I'd accepted defeat. We called it a day, finished our drinks and walked to the nearest Underground station to part ways.

Then, out of the blue, she held my hand. When we'd reached the station, she kissed me goodbye.

I was completely dumbfounded. I was certain she had no interest in me whatsoever. Nothing serious came of this date. We met a couple more times before realising we weren't compatible, but I'll never forget the lesson: stick with the game plan and try to build attraction as best you can.

If I'd given up after the first fifteen minutes and resigned myself to a friendly drink and nothing more, she would never have held my hand or kissed me. I'd learnt never to count myself out too early.

It doesn't matter how great you are at reading the signs, you're not a mind reader.

On another occasion, as a much younger man, the signs were there but I was too inexperience to read them. I'd flirted as best I could but couldn't gauge my date's interest in me. She'd agreed to a second date, which was more or less a repeat of the first. I'd flirted, nothing else happened, and she agreed to a third date. By the end of our third encounter I felt I had nothing else to lose and went in for a kiss.

She responded positively but immediately scolded me with a *"Finally!"* She warned me I'd taken far too long to kiss her and should have done so on the first date. She thought I wasn't interested in her and was starting to lose interest in me.

This was before I'd developed the attraction timeline model and learnt how to gauge interest and escalate properly. I'd discovered most women, no matter how much they like you, won't take the lead. As the man you have to take charge.

ATTRACTION TIMELINE

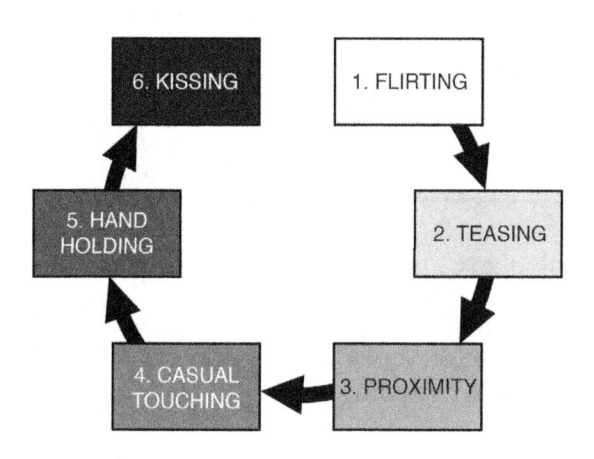

1. FLIRTING
2. TEASING
3. PROXIMITY
4. CASUAL TOUCHING
5. HAND HOLDING
6. KISSING

# After The First Date

No matter how well a first date goes with a woman, you haven't yet established a relationship with her. You'll have to meet *at least* twice before she'll consider suspending her internet dating profile and concentrating on you alone. Until that happens, her queue of interested men haven't disappeared. She may continue speaking to these suitors and even accept invites from them.

It's important to consolidate on a good first date with the following guidance. If not, her interest may wane and your blossoming relationship will be over before it's even begun.

**Post-First Date Messaging Strategy**

There's a crucial difference between your text messages before and after meeting a woman for the first time. Prior to a first date you were attempting to capture her attention, demonstrate your desirability, and build rapport. During this period you may have become prolific penpals, with phones buzzing eagerly throughout the day

After meeting in person the dynamic changes and text messaging often loses its appeal. Compared to the excitement of interacting face-to-face, tapping out lengthy texts all day is a poor substitute. You shouldn't expect, nor try, to maintain the same level of messaging you had prior to meeting.

Instead of those previous goals of capturing attention, demonstrating desirability, and building rapport, your post-first date messages must reflect the change in circumstance. Your new aims are twofold: to arrange a second date, and to ensure she doesn't lose interest.

Arranging a second date should be easy enough; simply agree a time and place to meet again. If your first date was a triumph, you may have already made those plans before parting ways. In this case simply confirm that arrangement via text. If you hadn't yet made those plans don't delay in asking to meet again. Unlike arranging a first date, there's no optimum time to ask (i.e. don't wait a couple of days before meeting). The sooner you confirm meeting again, the better. If you wait too long she may take that as a sign of indifference.

Ensuring she doesn't lose interest isn't so simple, especially if there's a lengthy wait before you're able to meet again. The solution here is counterintuitive and may seem like sabotage: you must give your date the opportunity to miss you and in doing so increase her desire to see you again.

The natural impulse after a successful first meeting is to escalate communication. This seldom ends well. You'll soon run out of things to say and the excitement of messaging each other will begin to fade. Her motivation to meet again will diminish, especially if she's speaking to other men in the meantime.

You must take your foot off the accelerator and allow her to set the pace of communication. If she continues to be highly invested in text messaging, then great, continue as you were - but in most cases she won't be. Don't be dismayed if contact suddenly declines. It's a normal part of transitioning from a virtual relationship to a real one.

If her messages begin to decrease in length and frequency, follow suit. Don't attempt to maintain her interest with regular, unprompted texts. You'll come across as needy for her attention - an unattractive look. Take a step back and save all that communication for the second date.

## The Second Date

*When* you meet again is often more important than what you plan on doing. If you wait too long before reuniting, the odds of a second date going well, or occurring at all, significantly decline. Absence does not make the heart grow fonder after a single date - it's more likely to extinguish a potential relationship.

In all instances, the sooner you meet again, the better. You will be able to pick up where you left off on the attraction timeline more comfortably; her interest in you wouldn't have dwindled due to prolonged absence; you wont have to alter your messaging strategy too drastically; and there won't be enough time for other men to make much headway in her queue.

If you can help it, wait no longer than a week to meet a second time. Any longer and it becomes difficult to maintain momentum. In the event of a triumphant first date (effortlessly completing the attraction timeline and creating a solid connection), suggest meeting the next day if possible. She'll be keen to see you again and begin establishing an exclusive relationship.

What you do for the second date depends entirely on how the first went. If you hadn't completed the attraction timeline, then that is your aim. Use the same strategy as before: multiple scenes with logistics conducive to escalating attraction. It's imperative you complete the attraction timeline before the end of a second date; if not with a kiss, at the very least hand-holding. If you're struggling to do so, there may not be a third date.

If you *had* completed the attraction timeline on the first date, your second meeting needn't be so prescriptive. Enjoying each other's company now takes precedence over building attraction, so there's less concern with logistics and multiple scenes. Taking a woman to an event or activity is often a great idea in this case. It takes the pressure off maintaining an interesting conversation.

## After the Second Date

After meeting twice, it should be clear if there's a relationship in the making or it's time to part ways. If she likes you but you're only halfway through the attraction timeline, you may be lucky enough to be given a third opportunity to reach the finish line - but don't count on it.

If there's no progress at all by the end of a second date, and it's not through lack of trying, it's time to cut your losses and accept she isn't attracted to you - no matter how friendly she's been or how much fun you've had together.

It's often upsetting when this happens. To have progressed so far with someone you like and for nothing romantic to come of it. As difficult as it may be, try not to become too emotionally involved until you know your feelings for a woman are reciprocated. As I'd mentioned in the Mastering Conversations chapter, it's prudent to not put all your eggs in one basket by exclusively speaking to one woman before you've received commitment from them. At any point before you both delete the dating apps and decide to 'go steady', your time together may abruptly end. Accept that as a fact of dating and get back on the internet wagon if/when it happens to you.

If you've reached the end of your second date having built attraction and established an obvious connection, there's no specific advice to take on your third, fourth, fifth meeting. Simply enjoy each other's company in whatever you both feel comfortable in doing. Build a bond together, have fun, and see what the future holds for the pair of you.

# General Dating Advice

You should now have a clear understanding of what a successful date looks like and how to create one. Below are a few additional pointers to ensure your dates go smoothly.

**First Date Ideas**

It may be cliché, but asking to meet for a coffee is always the best option when inviting a woman on a date. It's a non-committal, inexpensive opportunity to rendezvous before deciding to take things further. There's no obligation to extend the date for any longer than a drink if one of you doesn't feel it'll progress anywhere.

Alternatively, suggesting an alcoholic drink (singular) is fine, but only if you're meeting in the evening or know she's somewhat attracted to you (having built rapport via text messaging). Most women will avoid becoming tipsy and potentially vulnerable around a man she's never met before, so proposing a pub crawl is never a smart idea. Though once you've met for that initial drink, she may be quite happy to go bar hopping with you.

You may come across women online who decline coffee dates on the principle they're cheap and not worth their time. I've certainly read a few dating profiles with this disclaimer, usually followed by a list of 'acceptable' first date ideas. It should go without saying, this is a 'red flag' warning you to steer clear. There are a minority of women on dating sites less interested in finding love, and more interested in being wined, dined and entertained at your expense. They're usually easy to spot and avoid: anyone with a list of demands, expectations, or looking for 'a real man to spoil me' probably isn't great partner material.

## Who Pays?

The eternal dating dilemma: who should pay for a date? There is no universally accepted answer. You're partly damned if you do, and damned if you don't.

Some women are uneasy with the man covering costs. She doesn't want to feel she owes something in return, especially when there's no attraction. She may also feel strongly about equal partnerships and paying her own way - the thought of being subsidised could be infantilising.

Conversely, if the man doesn't pay for the date and they go halves instead, the woman may feel he's been unchivalrous. She may perceive it as a lack of generosity, or lack of resources to provide for her in the future. She may even feel disrespected, especially if she's a traditional type who believes the man should always pay on dates.

Given the strongly held opinions on both sides of this argument, there is never going to be a one-size-fits-all solution.

The best arrangement is to offer to pay for each expense during the first date; ensuring whatever you're doing isn't so extravagant. When meeting for that initial coffee, don't make a fuss, just pay for it. She may protest, but tell her it's fine - it's just a coffee.

If she's adamant she wants to go halves (or even pay for yours too), decline once, then acquiesce if she insists a second time. Don't be so stubborn as to cause an argument.

Most dates will accept the first drink and probably offer to pay for the next. When it's time for the next drink (hopefully at a new venue having changed scenes), go to pay again, but accept her offer if she wants to buy the second round.

If a venue is your idea, and a bit more expensive than a standard drink (e.g. a fancy cocktail bar, an activity, or a bite to eat) then you should pay. She may offer to pay her half, but decline once again unless she insists.

Meeting In Person

The point of the first date, besides getting to know each other, is to build attraction. How you deal with payment on a date can play an important role in this. So if you want to be seen as partner material, bite the bullet and open your wallet, unless she's adamant otherwise.

### Personal Experience

On one particular first date I'd met a woman for coffee. We approached the counter and ordered our drinks. I took out my wallet to pay.
My date already had her purse to hand and said she'd buy this round. I gestured to put her purse away: "It's fine, I've got this one." I told her.
"No, no, I'll get these." She replied.
I asked if she was sure. "Absolutely." She responded.

We were in a relationship for a couple of years after this meeting. Whenever the topic of dates came up, she never failed to remind me of that story - and to complain I didn't buy the first drinks.

At the time, If I'd argued it and insisted I pay, I would have come across as controlling and socially awkward. Because I didn't insist enough (by her reckoning), I was teased for being ungentlemanly for years after.
When it comes to dating etiquette, sometimes you just can't win. Don't be too hard on yourself for any faux pas - you can certainly recover from them, as I had in this case.

**Plan Ahead**

There's a happy medium when it comes to planning dates. On one hand, you can't create a detailed itinerary because dates are unpredictable. You must allow plenty of scope for spontaneity. But on the other hand, you can't leave the entire date in the lap of the gods. A lack of planning can ruin what may have been a great connection.

The secret is to find a starting location that's surrounded by quality venues - preferably ones you've scouted beforehand. Don't suggest meeting somewhere isolated, or a location you assume has lots to do nearby without knowing for sure that's true.

Town and city centres are always the best bet. There's often plenty to do within close proximity; transport links are greater; venues are typically open later; and women prefer to meet in populous places for safety reasons.

When it's time to change scenes, you should always know of a few nearby options to choose from. Winging it could result in you failing to find a decent venue and bring your date to a premature end.

### *Personal Experience*

I once hastily arranged a date within an hour of first contacting a woman. We got on great via messaging, but quickly discovered our calendars clashed and this was our only opportunity to meet for the foreseeable future.

She lived in a town a few miles away, so I'd offered to travel there to see her. I'd visited this place many times before and knew there were a few bars dotted around, so we wouldn't be short on things to do.

We met at a local landmark and then walked to a nearby pub. Due to a sporting event, the pub was packed beyond capacity. Standing room only, with a scrum of punters four deep to the bar. After slowly elbowing our way to the front, we'd ordered drinks.

After an uncomfortable twenty minutes stood at a packed venue, barely able to hear each other speak, we'd emptied our glasses and left the pub.

We walked around town looking for somewhere else to continue our date. Unfortunately it was a Sunday night, and many local venues had already closed for the evening. We finally came across the only place in town open: a snooker/pool hall.

I should have known immediately this was a mistake. We had to step over a sleeping homeless chap in the foyer to reach the entrance. After which a burly doorman ushered us into the building.

Once inside, my date visited the toilet. She returned to inform me all the cubical doors had been ripped off their hinges, allowing no privacy. The venue was rough around the edges to say the least. We'd ordered drinks at the bar and nursed them for an awkward fifteen minutes while the half dozen patrons sat in silence and watched us.

We left without finishing our drinks and I walked her to a nearby bus stop. We said our goodbyes and never spoke to each other again.
Although it's a comical looking back on how tragic that date's logistics were, it was genuinely awful at the time.

But I'd learnt my lesson - always plan ahead when it comes to venues.

## Take Charge

It's natural to encourage your date to make decisions. You'll want to come across as gentlemanly and considerate of her preferences, so letting her take the lead in where you go and what you do is an obvious way of doing this.

It may seem courteous and the right thing to do, but when constantly prompting your date to make decisions it demonstrates a few unattractive traits. It shows you are:

- Indecisive/afraid to make decisions in case you 'get it wrong'
- Unprepared, not knowing what to do next
- Desperate to please, eager to do anything she wants
- Boring, not caring enough to make decisions or having no preferences
- Irresponsible, avoiding accountability

Additionally, when relying on your date to make decisions you are burdening her with unwanted responsibility. She's on this date to be shown a good time and enjoy your company - not to become an impromptu event organiser.

So take charge of the date and demonstrate you're a confident and competent man. This means deciding when it's time for a change of scene, and where to go next. You needn't impose these decisions on her by diktat - ask her opinion, but make it easy and give options. For example, if you've just finished your initial coffee, instead of asking: *"Do you want to go somewhere else?"* try *"There's a cool gallery around the corner, fancy visiting?"*

Taking charge doesn't mean imposing your will. If your date doesn't want to move to a new location, or would rather go somewhere different to your suggestion, then no problem. Don't complain or try to change her mind, even in a lighthearted or jokey fashion.

Similarly, don't insist on making personal decisions for her, like what to eat or drink. This isn't attractive masculine behaviour, it's controlling and coercive.

## Pandering

As mentioned above, one of the reasons men won't take charge during dates is because they're eager to please. And we learn from a young age that if you want others to like you, it pays to be nice, accommodating and agreeable. When faced with an attractive woman, many men take this behaviour too far.

When seeking approval, our preferences, opinions and desires can quickly go out the window. You must guard against this and refrain from becoming overly agreeable. When you pander to your date, it's painfully obvious and unattractive.

Most women aren't looking for a people pleasing pushover. They want their partner to be a confident man, someone unashamedly himself and who doesn't compromise on his beliefs to gain favour from others

Not pandering doesn't mean becoming argumentative or domineering in some misguided attempt to impress women. It's simply about being honest with yourself and your date.

For example, if she reveals her love of hardcore electronic dance music and the clubbing scene, but that's your idea of hell, don't pretend you're a fan. Don't agree to go raving with her because you think that's what she wants to hear.

The key to avoiding pandering, and being honest with yourself and others, is to accept you're not going to be everyone's cup of tea. Don't radically change who you are to cater to your date's preferences and wants. If you and a date are incompatible for whatever reason, don't fight it. Accept and move on.

## Home Isn't Where The Heart Is

Women are justifiably cautious when meeting with men they don't yet know. Prior to any date, in the forefront of their mind is personal safety. For this reason, and a whole list of others, never suggest hosting a first date at your home. It doesn't matter if you live in a mansion, are a professional chef with impressive culinary skills, or have an extensive Fabergé egg collection you're keen to show off. The last thing a woman wants is to be stuck in a stranger's house if a date doesn't go well.

Meeting In Person

In addition to safety concerns, you'll be judged negatively if you invite a woman to your home for a first date. It suggests:

- You're lazy and can't be bothered to leave the house to meet her
- You're entitled and expect her to do all the travelling and come to you
- You're stingy and reluctant to pay for even a coffee, let alone other activities
- You're only interested in sex and are hoping to take this first date quickly to the bedroom

Even without those factors, from a logistics standpoint, your home is a terrible date location. You can't change scenes when stuck in one house, which makes if difficult to keep things interesting and build attraction.

So as a rule, never suggest meeting at your home for a first date.

## Chapter Summary

- Successful dates require ideal logistics. These include: no restrictive time constraints on your time together, you must be able to freely communicate verbally and non-verbally to each other, and the date must be held at an enjoyable environment for both parties.

- Just like a movie, a date must comprise multiple scenes to remain interesting and engaging. It's also necessary in building attraction.

- Each scene is preferably a new location, but can be a different activity/spot within the same location.

- Building attraction is the process of creating a romantic connection. It follows a particular timeline: verbal/body behaviour flirting, teasing, proximity and touching, and finally kissing.

- Only move on to each new stage of the timeline once you've gauged your date is comfortable/reciprocating at that level. If not, remain there or go back a stage.

- The aim during a first date is to complete this attraction timeline. If unsuccessful, continue into a second date.

- After a first date, arrange to meet again as soon as possible to continue momentum and establish a relationship.

- After two dates, it should be clear if a relationship is in the making, or it's time to go your separate ways.

PART 6

# Dating Mastery

```
        /\
       /  \
      / 5. \
     /MEETING\
    /IN PERSON\
   /------------\
  / 4. MESSAGING \
 /    STRATEGY    \
/------------------\
/  3. ONLINE DATING \
/--------------------\
/    2. BECOMING A    \
/    DESIRABLE MAN     \
/------------------------\
/  1. WHAT DO WOMEN WANT  \
```
(Pyramid diagram with side label "6. DATING MASTERY")

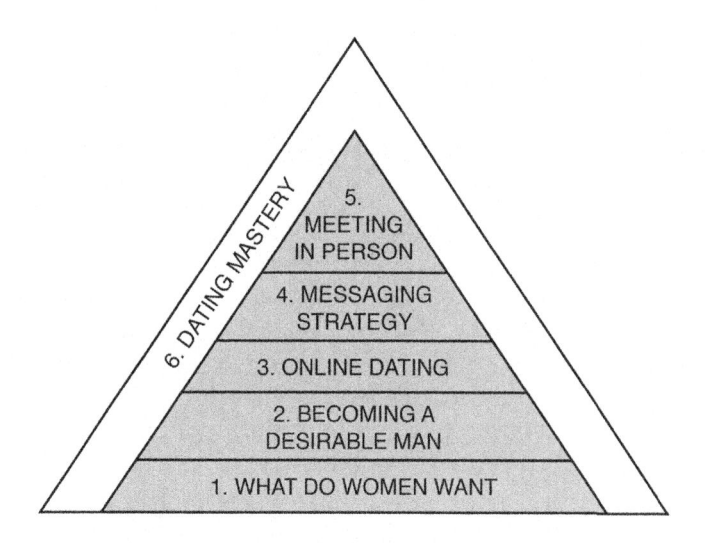

> *"We can be knowledgable with another man's knowledge, but we cannot be wise with another man's wisdom."*
>
> Michel de Montaigne
> renaissance philosopher and essayist

It's one thing to learn the contents of this book, but quite another to successfully apply it. It will take plenty of practice, frustration and failure before you become truly confident in yourself, and your ability to attract the opposite sex.

Becoming a desirable man is a longterm endeavour, not something achieved over a weekend. The same goes for your competency with dating. Garnering responses from women, arranging meetings, and building attraction are all skills you must work at. And like any skill, you may be clumsy to begin with, but with perseverance and regular practice, you can become quite adept.

In this chapter, I'll share with you a few final words of wisdom to help you on that journey - beginning by debunking some terrible dating advice.

# Terrible Dating Advice

There is a plethora of dating advice available, but how do you discern the good from the bad, the useful from the useless? It's not so easy when recommendations seem common sense, or have been around for generations and are unquestionably accepted. Below are a few common dating ideas to avoid - no matter how often you've heard them.

### Movie Magic

For many, first dates and cinemas are synonymous. It's *the* place to invite a woman when you want to pursue something romantic. And it's obvious why people think so: you're sat next to each other; there's a semblance of privacy in the dark; and with a moment's courage you can put your arm around her shoulders and kindle a relationship.

The reality is completely different. If your entire date revolves around sitting in silence next to a woman, then you're in trouble. There's no opportunity to communicate, to enjoy each other's company, or to build attraction. If you're hoping to get physical, there's no way of slowly escalating. You can't test her reaction to proximity or use casual touching though multiple scenes before holding hands. From a cinema seat, your only option is to go from zero to a hundred and hope for the best.

So don't risk it. Only see a movie with a woman if you've already built attraction and are at the physical stage. Otherwise you're wasting precious time together that should be spent developing a connection.

## Dinner Dates

Picture a romantic first date and what image springs to mind? The archetype would be a candlelit dinner for two at some quaint restaurant. Getting to know someone over a meal is the definitive date activity. When looking for love, it's almost a rite of passage to dress up, go somewhere fancy, and embarrass yourself by mispronouncing foreign dishes to an unimpressed waiter.

Despite its popularity, inviting a woman for dinner is a terrible idea for a first date. It presents a whole gamut of potential issues to deal with: dietary restrictions; anxiety around eating in front of others; allergies; preferring not to speak whilst dining; irritable bowel syndrome and other issues prompted by food; not wanting to be judged for choosing the 'wrong' dishes; deciding who pays for the meal, and so on and so on.

Now include the limitations of being stuck at one venue during a date. The atmosphere may not be comfortable, you may not be afforded privacy, communication may be difficult, it may be impossible to escalate physically when building attraction...

Going for a meal during a first date is only advisable when it happens naturally during the course of your time together and isn't the main event. If you meet for a coffee, then walk around a park, visit a museum, get a few drinks and *then* decide to visit a restaurant, then great go for it. By that point you've already spent a few hours together, changed scenes, became acquainted and hopefully built attraction. You can also choose together where to eat, and there's no pressure on the meal being an important part of the date's itinerary.

So think twice before asking: *"Would you like to go for dinner some time?"* - you may be ruining your chances of a successful date before you've even had it.

## Feminine Pursuits

Internet dating aside, if you want to meet women outside of your work and social circles, where do you turn? A common suggestion is to partake in new interests or hobbies that are predominately female. This way you're guaranteed to meet plenty of women and increase your odds of finding that someone special.

On paper this makes sense. It's a much easier way to meet women compared to striking up conversations with strangers at bars. But is it an effective use of your time and energy? Joining a group of women in the hopes of forming a relationship with one of them is a very optimistic gamble.

Let's say you take up salsa dancing looking for love. Salsa is a partnered style, where traditionally the man leads his female partner through a routine. Its classes are famously oversubscribed with women. Join any session and you'll be in demand as one of the few chaps there.

Now imagine you're the only man in a class of thirty women. Those are great odds, right? Not on closer inspection. How many of those women are going to be single? Of those, how many are going to be attracted to you? Of these, how many are you attracted to? It's not improbable to find the answer is 'none'. And how long would it have taken you to discover this? Unlike internet dating, you can't gauge someone's relationship status and interest in you in seconds.

There are other factors that make this strategy a poor choice. Firstly, it may be painfully obvious what your ulterior motive is. When some overweight, middle-aged man with absolutely no interest or previous experience in dance takes up salsa, you know what he's there for.

Secondly, being the only man amongst a group of women doesn't automatically make you desirable to them. This isn't some post-apocalyptic scenario where you're one of the few men available to these women; outside of salsa class they still have plenty of options.

I'm not suggesting you never take up what's considered a feminine activity or pastime - but be honest with yourself and your motivations. If you have a genuine interest in yoga, flower arranging, or feminist political activism, then by all means get involved. But if deep down you know it's just a ploy to meet women and you wouldn't be so keen if the participants were exclusively men, then spend your time and energy elsewhere.

## You Don't Bring Me Flowers

When meeting for the first time, it's tradition to bring your date a gift. This usually means flowers or chocolates, but can involve something a bit more thoughtful: a book on a particular subject she's interested in, or some relevant trinket if she collects them.

Gifts can be a great ice breaker and show you're romantic, generous, and thoughtful. But there are plenty of reasons to avoid gifts on a first date.

From a purely practical perspective, once you've handed over the present, your date is obligated to carry it around and look after it for the duration of your time together. If that's a bouquet of flowers, it can prove to be a pain - especially if you end up moving from place to place over a few hours.

And with flowers especially, there's also the potential for embarrassment. It may be a clear signal to others nearby that you're on a first date, prompting the more nosy types to take notice. No one wants to draw unnecessary attention to themselves on a date. Most of us will be self-conscious enough without worrying about providing unwitting entertainment for eavesdroppers.

Flowers aside, no matter what the gift, it may not be taken in the spirit intended. Gifts are much like compliments: how they're received depends greatly on who's giving them. If a woman finds you desirable, it will be seen as a lovely gesture. But when meeting for the first time, she hasn't yet made up her mind about you.

If she doesn't feel some instant attraction, an introductory gift may be seen as a cheap attempt to buy her affection. She may also be uncomfortable accepting as she will feel obliged to return the favour somehow - not a position she'll want to be in for a man she isn't attracted to.

So like compliments, don't give gifts until you know they'll be welcomed and appreciated. If you feel inclined, bring a small present on the second date, only if you've successfully built attraction. Better yet, wait until you're visiting her home for the first time; by this point flowers are an excellent idea.

> ### *Personal Experience*
> Occasionally I've received complaints about a lack of flowers or other first date gifts. When this happens I never apologise or make excuses.
> Instead I'll explain, with tongue in cheek, that where I'm from it's actually tradition for the women to bring a gift on a first date... and I'm quite upset by *my* lack of flowers.
>
> In my experience, this complaint from women is always a lighthearted tease. During one first date it became such a running joke that I took her to Kew Gardens for our second meeting, so she could look at as many flowers as she wanted (while I steadfastly refused to gift her any).
>
> So if you hear this complaint, play along and flirt back - don't treat it as a serious grievance.
> But on the off chance your date really is upset by a lack of gift, consider it 'red flag' and proceed accordingly.

### "How you doin'?"

Chat up lines are not magical incantations with the power to enchant women. Unfortunately some men believe otherwise, and are convinced they're a great way to impress the opposite sex - if only you can find the right words.

Approaching a stranger and introducing yourself with a risqué/cheesy opener will only work if two criteria are met: the woman on the receiving end is sufficiently attracted to you, and she's in the mood to entertain your advances. It's as simple as that. The chat up line itself is almost irrelevant. If you're deemed undesirable, or it's an inappropriate time to 'make your move', you'll be politely (or not so politely) brushed off.

So unless you're confident in knowing you're the right man at the right time, don't expect miracles when informing a stranger her dress looks good, but would look better on your bedroom floor.

### Can't Buy Me Love

A man's desirability depends on numerous criteria. Women evaluate us by our health, fitness, strength, grooming, dress, wealth, career, confidence, intelligence, life experience, facial features, height, social status... and a whole list of other attributes that make us who we are.

It's a complex assessment that weighs up the pros and cons of a man, and measures them against a woman's wants and preferences. In a nutshell, if you tick enough of her boxes she'll be attracted to you - if not, she won't.

Plenty of men are oblivious to this subconscious process and don't understand what it is exactly women find attractive. It's this group who rely on an age-old courtship strategy: attempting to buy affection.

This means gifts, expensive dates, grand romantic gestures, and even handing over cash - all in an attempt to make a woman like them.

And it can work... to a degree. Women are attracted to men who can provide, and showering someone with gifts certainly fulfils that criterion. But if that generosity isn't backed up with other desirable traits, her interest will wane very quickly indeed, assuming it was ever there at all.

Most women are not swayed by gifts. This shouldn't come as a surprise because neither are you. If an ugly woman attempted to buy your affection by taking you out for expensive meals or gifting you nice things, would it work? Of course not. If you were an unscrupulous type, maybe you'd accept the generosity and entertain the woman just long enough to not be considered rude or ungrateful, but it wouldn't change how you felt towards her.

If you're thinking of opening your wallet in an attempt to impress a woman, reconsider. That money is much better spent on yourself: go travelling, pay for a qualification to further your career prospects, or buy a new outfit. Each of these investments in yourself will increase your desirability far more than any gift could.

### Personal Experience

I was once in a relationship with a woman named Mary who owned a beautiful necklace. It was her favourite adornment and she wore it every special occasion. Mary proudly told me it was from Tiffany & Co jewellers and cost around a month's salary... but the best part was, she got it for free.

Long before we had met, an older work colleague of Mary's had taken a shining to her. He expressed his feelings, begged to take her out on a date and promised her the earth. She wasn't interested in the slightest, and so politely informed him - multiple times.

After supposedly accepting this and agreeing to keep things platonic, one day the colleague came into work with a gift for Mary. There was no occasion; it wasn't her birthday nor had she achieved anything worth celebrating. The colleague just wanted to give her a present to show how much Mary's friendship meant to him.

Mary refused the necklace, knowing just how expensive it was, and suspecting an ulterior motive behind the gift. The colleague was insistent she take it; he was adamant it was purely platonic, there were no strings attached, and he would be offended if she refused.

So she took the necklace and enjoyed it ever since. Mary left that job shortly after and never spoke to the former work colleague again.

Was this an innocent gift between friends? Of course not. Had Mary been a man, would this work colleague even dream of spending a month's salary on a gift for them? Never.

After failing to convince Mary to date him, he hoped an extravagant display of generosity would change her mind. It didn't, and it was never going to, no matter how expensive the offering.

Don't make the same mistake Mary's work colleague had - you can't buy a woman's desire.

### Pursue and Persist

If a romantic gesture doesn't win a woman over, what will? How about another gesture? Then another, and another, and another - until finally you've accrued enough 'love points' before she changes her mind.

Men can waste their entire lives pursuing women in this fashion in the hope of reciprocated love. They believe a woman's affection can be earned with perseverance and determination. That relationships are formed by proving to a woman how serious they are about them, and how great a partner they'd be.

Although misguided, it's a common mindset amongst men, and for a few reasons.

Firstly, like a lot of the 'terrible dating advice' in this chapter, it's borne of common sense. In almost every other aspect of life, if you're persistent with something and work on it, you can achieve your goals. Wooing a woman should be no different, right? If you persevere, make your feelings known and prove what a catch you are, you'll eventually win her over.

Secondly, cast your mind back to one of the first concepts in this book: attraction isn't a choice. Our attraction to other people is an unconscious, unwitting feeling. Plenty of men don't understand this and assume they can negotiate or reason with a woman's feelings, convincing her to feel desire. They believe through persistence, a woman can be persuaded into loving them.

And thirdly, the reason this idea is so prevalent is due in part to the media we consume. It's the Disney-fication of love stories - where a man eventually wins the love of an uninterested woman by proving his worthiness. It's a common trope, and one we all grow up watching and believing is the correct way to earn a woman's affection.

Pursuing an apathetic woman over weeks, months, or even years doesn't work. She won't reciprocate your desire once you've performed enough meaningful acts, or proven how strong your feelings are.

At best this method will convince a reluctant woman to be with you, but only if she doesn't have any better options. From her perspective, being with you is better than nothing, but there won't be any genuine desire for a relationship - just permission for it to happen.

Instead of pursuing and persisting with averse women, you ought to be putting that time and effort into improving yourself. Work on becoming a desirable man and attract women who are enthusiastic to be with you.

## Befriend Before Betroth

Should you become friends with a woman before attempting to woo her? It's a popular school of thought: you must develop a platonic relationship before attempting a romantic one.

There are two arguments for this advice.
The first is cautionary wisdom from a bygone age, when couples married in their teens and divorce was hard to come by. If you're going to be legally bound to someone for the rest of your days, you'd better be sure you *can* be friends and it isn't just physical attraction driving the engagement.

But now times have changed and relationships aren't so prescriptive. There's no pressure to commit to someone for life before even living with them. If things don't work out because you're not compatible, it's much easier to separate and there's no taboo over doing so. Most people have multiple relationships before finding 'the one' and settling down, so there's no pressure to get it right first time.

The second argument comes from a misunderstanding of how attraction works. Some men believe friendship is a prerequisite to a woman developing *true* feelings for a man. Without friendship, a woman's liking is just shallow interest based on physical appearance only.

This is nonsense men tell themselves when unsuccessful in attracting strangers: "*If she knew the* real *me, she'd see what a great guy I am…*"

This isn't true of course. Women are quite capable of determining a man's desirability the first time they meet. It isn't necessary to know someone for months, or years, before a his 'true value' becomes apparent.

So befriending women before attempting to court them is unnecessary *and* irrational, but it can also be counterproductive. If you've been secretly pining for a female friend and then decide to make your true feelings known, how'd you think she'll react? Best case scenario, she secretly feels the same way but was too afraid to act. But it's more than likely she has no romantic desire towards you whatsoever. If she had, it would have probably been obvious by now - if not from her own actions, then from mutual friends letting you know.

After changing the dynamic by becoming flirtatious suddenly, or confessing your feelings outright, your friend will probably feel awkward and upset.

She'll feel deceived that you'd used a platonic friendship to get close to her with ulterior motives, and will be justified in thinking the friendship was a sham - that you weren't interested in her as person, but only as a potential partner.

The most likely outcome from this will be ruining the friendship and failing miserably at converting it into something romantic.

So don't befriend a woman in the hopes of wooing her later. Her desire for you won't increase over time or proximity. No matter how long you've known her, or how close you become, she'll think of you as a friend and nothing more. If you want to build attraction and pursue something romantic, do so from the very beginning.

### Soliciting Strangers

Online dating has plenty of detractors, and justifiably so. Many can't make a success of it due to the time, effort and knowhow required - but approaching women in the 'real world' is not always a viable alternative.

I've often heard variations on *"I don't understand why anyone uses Tinder - if you like the look of someone, just go over and say hello."*
I'm not suggesting this method doesn't work - after all, it's been propagating the human race since we began living in settlements. But there is a time and a place for it: when you and the woman in question are both out socialising.

Any time outside of this window, and chances are the woman who's caught your attention just wants to be left alone. The interruptions some women face from men when out in public are constant. To avoid these unwelcome approaches women will: go about their business at quieter times of day to avoid men; wear headphones (with or without music playing) to be left undisturbed; avoid going out alone, as men prefer targeting solitary women when making advances.

What if a woman is being friendly and doesn't seem to mind speaking to you? It depends on the circumstances. If she's at work and serving you in some capacity, then she's obligated to be friendly and chat - more so if there's gratuity on the line. That isn't a sign she's interested in you.

Women will also entertain some men's advances in order to avoid confrontation. If she feels her personal safety is on the line, she's unlikely to tell a man outright she isn't interested and to go away. Often it's prudent to just grin and bear it for a couple of minutes.

So if you're at a bar or something and see someone you like the look of, by all means pluck up the courage and introduce yourself. But outside of a socialising environment, it's not often a wise move.

### You'll Find Love Once You Stop Looking For It

Imagine being stranded in the Australian Outback. Supplies are dwindling and if you don't find water soon you're in trouble. You thumb through a survival guide looking for help out of this life-threatening situation. Reaching the chapter on procuring drinking-water, you read: *"You'll find water once you stop looking for it."*

You'd have to be delirious from dehydration before that advice makes sense. The same goes when looking for a partner: your 'special someone' isn't hiding around some corner, waiting for you to stop looking before they jump out to surprise you.

If you want to find love, you have to work for it. Not retreat back from the search and hope that by ignoring your singledom hard enough, an interested partner will land in your lap. Follow the guidance in this book: become a desirable man, and work on attracting women online and dating them. This will yield results - burying your head in the sand will not.

## Fishing For Feedback

Feedback is essential for improvement. If you're not aware of your shortcomings, how do you hope to correct them? When attempting to master the dating game, it makes sense to seek out constructive criticism - and who better to ask than the women you've failed to attract?

It's tempting to enquire 'what went wrong' when a woman decides you're not the one for her; especially if you've been messaging for a while, or have even met up for a date or two. But you must resist the urge to seek closure and ask for feedback - because you're never going to get it, at least not *explicitly*.

Feedback is only useful if it's accurate and honest, but when it comes to justifying our decisions in matters of the heart, that's seldom the case.

It's very unlikely a woman is going to be forthright on why she doesn't want to be with you. Whatever answer she gives will shaped by two subconscious aims: to avoid upsetting or angering you, and avoid any negative judgement towards herself.

So you won't hear the brutal truth... that she thought you were too short, had an awful haircut, didn't earn enough money, and she has another date lined up this weekend with a more desirable man.
Instead you'll get the easy-to-swallow version: *"It's not you, it's me"*, *"I think we'd be better as friends"*, *"We're just not compatible"* etc.

So don't bother asking - it's awkward for her, and pointless for you.

As you can't get *explicit* feedback, you have to rely on the *implicit* kind. It's reading between the lines, using a bit of detective work to uncover where you're going wrong. Look for emerging patterns: if you keep failing at the same stage (e.g. no worries getting first dates, but can't build attraction) then that's where your attention should be. Don't ask her what you didn't get right, figure it out by yourself.

If you've been implementing the guidance in this book, that shouldn't be such a struggle. Compare what I've recommended with what you're actually doing. If you deviate too far from the path I've mapped out, that's where you need to get back on track.

When you fail, and you will many times, don't take it to heart and don't take it too seriously. You may not have done anything wrong at all. Remember 'The Queue' and how it shapes a woman's behaviour beyond what you can see. A more attractive prospect may have caught your date's eye. But that's life - don't dwell on it, use that disappointment to spur you on.

## Embracing Failure

There's only one route to success: failure. The strategies and guidance in this book didn't come to me in a dream. A burning bush didn't advise me how to create an attractive dating profile, or what to message a woman, or where to take her on a date. All of that I had to learn the hard way - by first getting it wrong.

And I had to get it wrong over and over again, until I figured out how to get it right.

This book provides the best shortcut to becoming a desirable man and attracting an amazing partner, but that's not to say it'll be easy. You still have to put the work in, and that means overcoming constant failures. You'll fail to get responses to messages. You'll fail to get conversations going. You'll fail to get dates. You'll fail to hold a woman's attention. You'll fail to build attraction.

It'll be awkward, embarrassing, and even upsetting - but that's the route you must take to achieve this goal. So don't shy away from it. Really embrace failure, lean into it and learn to fail a little less each time. Only then can you succeed.

It will be worth it. In six months/a year/five years from now, you will be in the best shape of your life: mentally, physically, emotionally and romantically.
You'll look back and think "*It was hard at the time, but I'm so glad I did it.*"

So hang in there, stick with it, and do yourself proud. I know you can do it, because I did.

## Take A Break

"*You must understand that the workout does not actually produce muscular growth. The workout is merely a trigger that sets the body's growth mechanism into motion. It is the body itself, of course, that produces growth; but it does so only during a sufficient rest period.*"

    Mike Mentzer
    'Mr Olympia' world champion bodybuilder

When it comes to building muscle, the rest days between workouts are just as important as the workouts themselves. It's during this time the body is able to repair itself and become stronger than before. If you were to weight train seven days a week, you'll become increasingly tired and any potential gains in strength and muscle mass will grind to a halt.

Rest is an integral part to improving your strength - and the same goes for improving your dating game.

To succeed you must embrace failure, but that failure will eventually take its toll. Not physically, but emotionally. Constant rejection, over an extended period will adversely affect your mental health. Your self worth will ebb away and eventually you'll become hurt and resentful.

Long before you get to that stage, you must take a break from online dating. Delete the apps and forget about them for a while. Concentrate on improving those important aspects of becoming a desirable man: good health, fitness, income, hobbies/interests, your happiness. Spend time with friends and enjoy yourself.

Then return to online dating feeling renewed and in slightly better shape than when you last used it. Repeat this process as often as you need to. Just as a bodybuilder rests between training days, you need to rest every so often between stints of sending messages and going on dates.

You'll find a rest frequency and duration that's right for you, but a good place to start is three weeks on, and one week off online dating. You may not need the rest initially, or you may fancy longer than a week off. There are no rules, it's whatever feels right for you. As you become more successful with online dating, the need for those breaks will decrease - it will feel less like a hard slog, and more like playing a game; one you're good at.

So don't be afraid to take regular breaks. It's not a sign of weakness, or a failing on your part - it's an essential part of a long term strategy to master dating.

# Exceptions To The Rule

It's impossible to write a book like this without making frequent, sweeping generalisations.

But it should go without saying, womankind isn't some homogeneous hive mind who all think, feel and react the same way in every circumstance. For every explanation, strategy, or process I've shared, there will always be instances where they don't work or apply. These few exceptions tend to prove the rule, however.

A common example are women actively engaged in a particular subculture. This could be anything from a religion, to environmental activism, to punk, to bohemianism. In short, any special interest that encompasses an entire lifestyle and isn't just a hobby.

You could be eminently desirable to most women, but a born-again Christian or vegan or Harley-Davidson biker probably isn't going to be interested in a partnership unless you already participate in their lifestyle.

There's little to be done in these scenarios, except acknowledge you can't be everyone's cup of tea. The alternative is to adopt an entire subculture with its activities, principles, and beliefs in an attempt to attract just one woman. If you're ever tempted to go down this path, just remember: pandering is never attractive.

So when you come across exceptions where the usual rules don't apply for whatever reason, either adopt your strategy if you think it's worth your while, or cut your losses and move on.

# Notes To A Young Man

If you're currently in your late teens/early twenties and struggling, these words are for you.

At that age I could sum up my love life in one word: nonexistent. I was very much single and felt things would stay that way indefinitely. The few girls I knew had no interest in me, while male friends seemed to have no trouble attracting them. I didn't know what I was doing wrong, or how to improve my situation. This failure to get any kind of romantic attention made me think there was something wrong with me - that I was inherently unattractive.

I often heard people say that period should be the 'happiest years of your life', but they weren't for me. I was lonely and felt helpless about it.

If this resonates, I want to reassure you with a couple of points.

- You are not alone in feeling this way. So many young men feel lonely, unloved and unloveable. You won't know that because men don't talk about their feelings or how they're doing - especially when they're struggling. Additionally, with social media and celebrity culture, it's now almost impossible to get a true measure of how you compare to others your age. If you believe everything you see on Instagram or 'reality' TV shows, they're all having the time of their lives - besides you. But that isn't the case. Don't compound your unhappiness by thinking you're alone, you aren't. What you're experiencing is completely normal and very common.

- There's a reason you're struggling with the opposite sex right now, and it has nothing to do with inexperience or any personal failings on your part. At this age, your overall desirability is at its lowest. Your ability to provide and protect is extremely limited, so unless you're physically attractive and can rely on good looks, things won't be so easy. Couple this with another fact: women around your age are currently at their peak desirability. You're not just competing for a girl's attention from other guys your age - but men of all ages. And those slightly older will have a huge advantage over you. But rest assured, this dynamic is temporary and will be over before you know it. In time you'll naturally become more desirable as you age and find your place in the world.

So it's normal to struggle, and there's a reason for it. Don't blame yourself or think you're failing miserably.

If things aren't great now, don't believe for a second they'll stay that way forever. No matter how dire your current circumstances, you have a precious gift that will help you improve your lot and achieve great things - autonomy.

For the first eighteen-odd years of life, you have minimal freedom. You'll wake up when told to, eat what you're given, live where your parents/guardians do, attend school, and be sent to bed long before you're tired.

As you approach adulthood, your life is no longer entirely dictated by others. Incrementally, you can decide what to do with your time, until eventually you're in charge.

Of course, you'll never have *complete* freedom: the ability to wake up each day and do *whatever* you want with the next 24 hours. We all have limitations, restrictions and obligations, but you'll have enough autonomy to make important decisions and steer your life in whatever direction you choose.

If you want to become a desirable man and attract the opposite sex, now's the time to exercise that autonomy. The decisions you make now can affect the rest of your life, for good or ill. So don't waste energy ruminating over how bad things are currently. Instead, use this time wisely to build the foundations of a successful future.

It's never too late to work on the following advice, but starting young can give you a life-changing advantage by the time you're in your 30s, 40s, 50s and beyond. Ask any older man, and they will wish they took this advice - or are glad they actually did.

## Health

Getting into great physical shape should be every young man's priority. Socrates said it best a couple thousand years ago: *"No man has the right to be an amateur in the matter of physical training. It is a shame for a man to grow old without seeing the beauty and strength of which his body is capable."*

Long before your metabolism slows down, and aches, pains and niggles are commonplace, make the most of your body. It's so much easier to get into shape and stay that way when you're younger. Incorporate some form of exercise into your daily routine, practice eating a sensible diet, and get plenty of sleep.

## Wealth

At this stage in life your earning potential is minimal. If you're working part-time around studies, or have a full-time 'entry level' role, you won't be able to accumulate much money. But there is one thing you can do now to ensure your future finances... avoid debt.

Some young men fall into the trap of living a high-income lifestyle on a low-income salary with the use of store cards, credit cards and payday loans. It may be fun for a while, but it isn't sustainable. Best case scenario, you max out a modest credit limit and must pay it back over the next year or so.

But worst case, you spiral into serious debt, borrowing from new lenders to pay back previous ones. Then being taken to court because you can't keep up with repayments and having your possessions seized. Finally being placed under restrictive repayment plans for years or even decades.

Debt can rob you of your freedom. Don't hinder your opportunities later in life because of a few bad financial decisions now.

### Social Circle

The friendships you foster are life's true riches. As raconteur Quentin Crisp quipped: *"If I am rich, it is because I have taken my wages in people."* You really cannot have enough friends. Those closest to you will shape your life and enrich it in so many ways. Not just through companionship, but by offering support, guidance and opportunities.

You'll often hear *"It's not what you know, but who you know"* when it comes to success. Talent and hard work can often go unrewarded if you're not friends with the right people. So to avoid that from occurring, whilst you're young and regularly meeting new people, work on expanding your social circle.

Take up invites to socialise, try new things and broaden your horizons. You'll be grateful you did later in life. Compared to improving your health and finances, making new and deep friendships can be most challenging as you get older. Besides a few workmates, many older men have no real friends at all. So avoid that fate by getting out there now and make a habit of meeting new people and making friends.

Remember that becoming a desirable man is a longterm project. Don't think harshly of yourself because the first years of adulthood are difficult. Stick with it and instead look forward to an exciting future. I achieved great success by following the advice in this book - you will too.

# What Is Dating Mastery?

Mastering the dating game isn't the ability to attract *every* woman. It's not about becoming so handsome that women double take in the street, or your presence alone makes them weak at the knees.

It's also not about getting responses to every message sent, or dates from every conversation, or completing the attraction timeline at each attempt.

In short, dating mastery isn't the absence of failure; It's actually your relationship to it and your relationship with success. Dating mastery is:

- Understanding and accepting that your failures will far outnumber your successes
- Recognising when you're responsible for your failures - and more importantly, when you're not
- Learning from and improving upon those failures
- Understanding what it takes to succeed and striving towards that
- Being confident in your ability to attract women: not through wishful thinking, but from a solid track record of previous successes
- Knowing that your hard work pays off, and that failures today pave the way to successes tomorrow

Dating mastery isn't an achievement, but a state of being. It's a mindset developed by playing the dating game and sticking with it. You'll note it isn't just the peak of the 'Dating Knowledge Pyramid', it encases all of it and is developed at every stage.

To borrow from Rudyard Kipling, with enough practice and experience, you will be able to "...*meet with Triumph and Disaster, and treat those two imposters just the same...*"

In time, dating disasters won't phase you, and the triumphs won't surprise you.

# Epilogue

This book maps a journey. The route taken will be different for each reader, but the destination is the same: to meet someone special, love them, and be loved in return.

For some men, the journey is short and straightforward. For others, it's a more lengthy and difficult path. If you find yourself in the latter camp, don't be disheartened. It just makes the destination that much sweeter when you get there - and I have every confidence you will get there.

Before you embark on that path, thank you for buying my book. If you've found it useful, please consider leaving a review. I read all feedback online and it means a great deal to me knowing I've been of some help to you.

Best of luck on your journey, I wish you every success!

Printed in Great Britain
by Amazon